ABSOLUTE BEGINNERS

The Most Complete Guide
to Learning Crochet Effortlessly
With Step-by-Step and Illustrated Instructions,
Beginner-Friendly Patterns and Fun Project Ideas.

GRACE MAYERS

TABLE OF CONTENTS

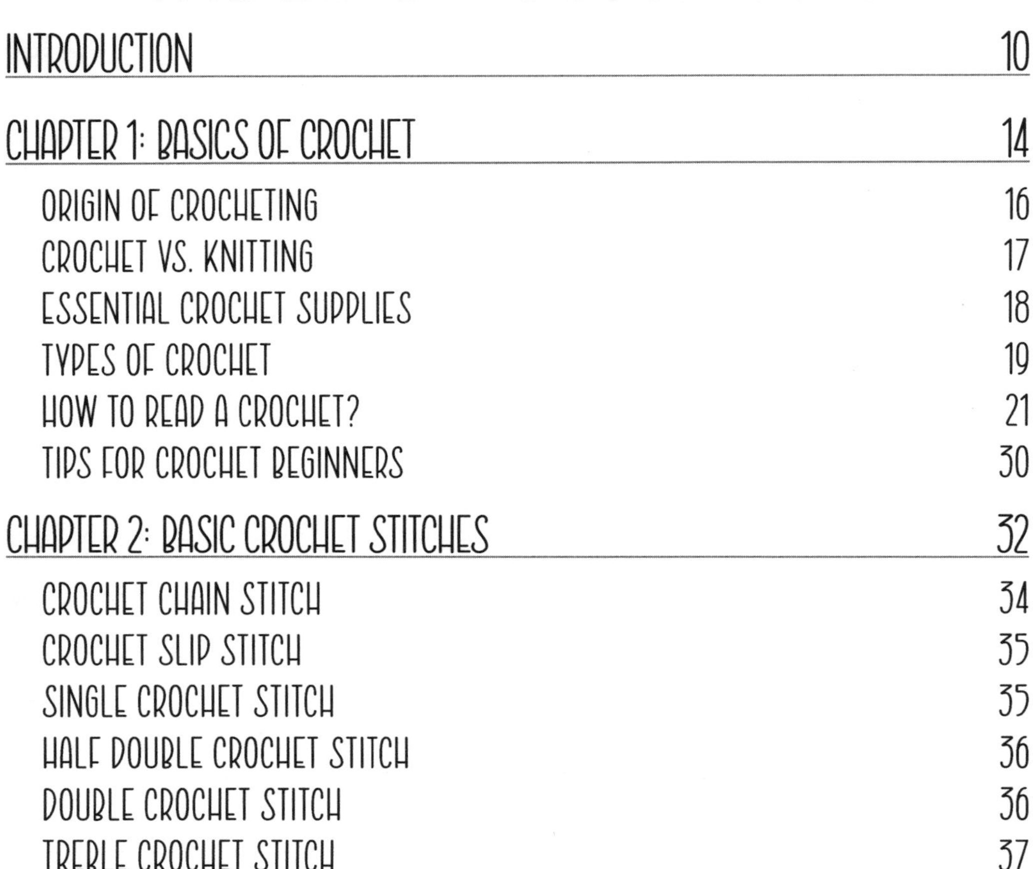

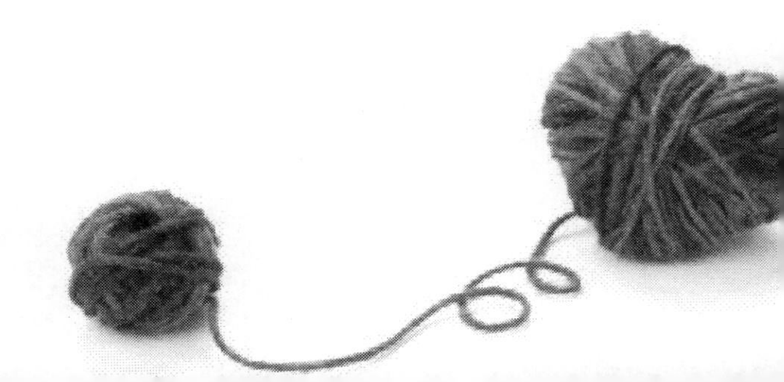

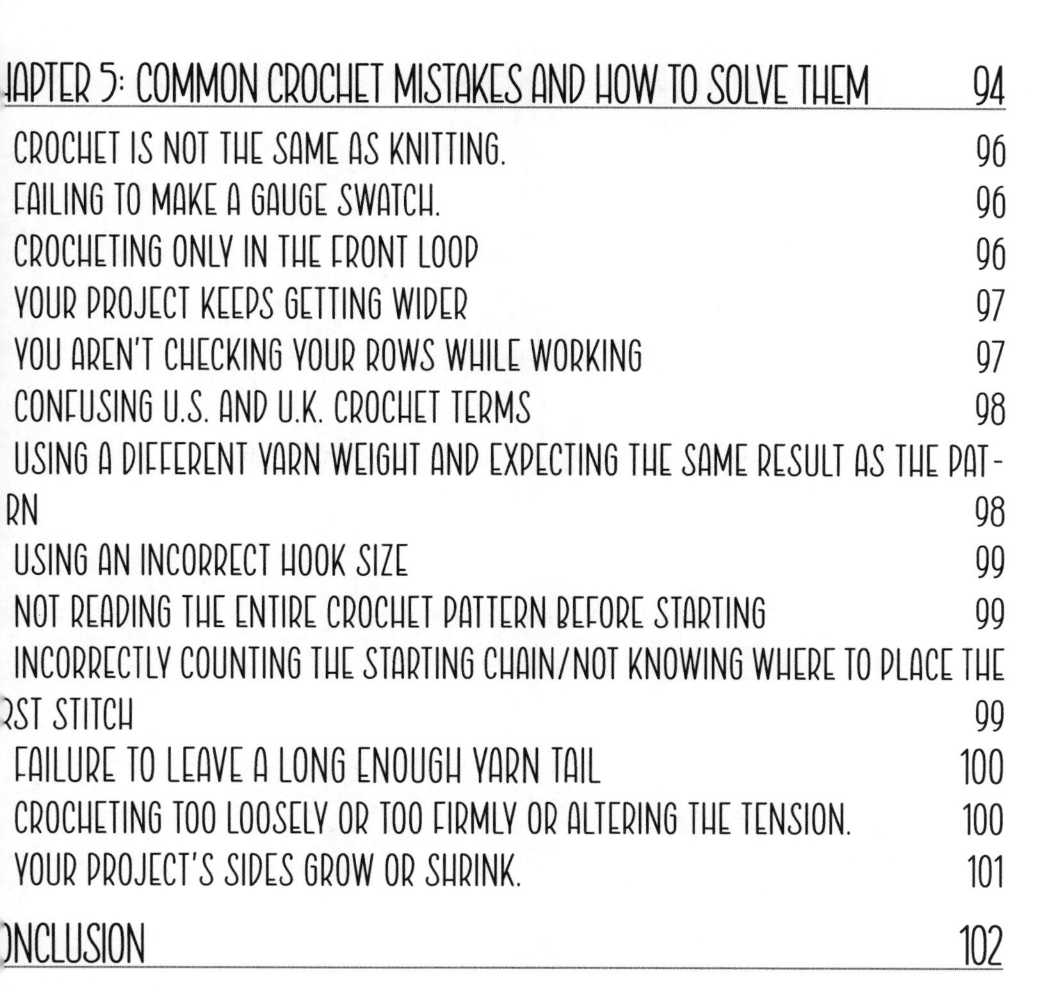

INTRODUCTION

Crocheting serves as a form of mental and physical healing and a source of many love- items. It's a fantastic activity that's both enjoyable and beneficial. Crochet is a technique at uses a crochet pin to create yarn or crochet threads. Crochet is a term that means ook.' Simply starting with a knot, place the crochet hook into the loop, coil the hook, and aw it through the first loop for starting a crochet Project. Wrap the yarn around the hook nd draw it into the final loop until it reaches the desired length. Because each loop pass- s through the preceding loop, it is referred to as a chain. After the chains are created, a rcle is made by working in rounds by joining the final chain with a slip knot, or the chains an be turned and worked in rows. When working in rows, the task is turned at the end of ach row, and when working in rounds, the job may be switched on or off at any time. The atterns will tell you when and when not to change. A thread is formed when the yarn is rapped around crochet thread, and one or more loops are drawn through the preceding w's or circle's chain or stitches. The best part about Crochet is that just one active loop ays on the hook at the end of each thread.

rocheting may be used to make a variety of clean fabrics, such as doilies, tablecloths, nd bedspreads. Tops, sweaters, shawls, skirts, scarves, hats, headbands, socks, and ippers may all be customized. Additional crocheted goods include container clothes, tow- s, mats, and napkins. Crochet may be used to create an infinite variety of crafts. The best art is that your creations can be used around the house or given as presents. Crocheting more than simply a pastime; it offers several advantages. Learning many crafts or hobbies can be rather costly. Crocheting isn't that expensive. Crocheting is a highly appealir pastime to learn since the supplies necessary to get started are relatively basic and ine: pensive.

Learning to Crochet entails being acquainted with a restricted number of increasing stitcl es. After you've mastered these fundamentals, starting a little project may be simple ar non-threatening. Always remember to begin with something simple and practical. You need to learn how to create chains, single crochet, and double Crochet, so practice thes stitches until you're comfortable with them. Don't quit if they don't turn out correctly for tl first time; it just takes some practice. As soon as it started feeling comfortable for you wi the basics of crocheting, you would be able to start practically any project you want. An e: plosion will occur, resulting in creating your headgear, scarves, blankets, and other item Only the most difficult ones should be left behind. Among the most vital and valuable thinç to accomplish are to get baby goods. Do you imagine the money you'll save by creatir quality and inexpensive gifts for the entire family? Who doesn't appreciate unique han crafted items, such as a wide scarf or a cozy hat? Crocheting is a rewarding activity sinc it allows you to be confident and comfortable. Your crochet masterpieces will be praise and complimented by your loved ones. When you learn to crochet, you will pass on yo knowledge to people around you. Crocheting is an easy, enjoyable, and helpful activit The most significant part is that you can create several projects for your home.

House, family, and friends may all be had for a minimal price. Crocheting is a lovely sk that should be handed down from generation to generation.

Let's get started.

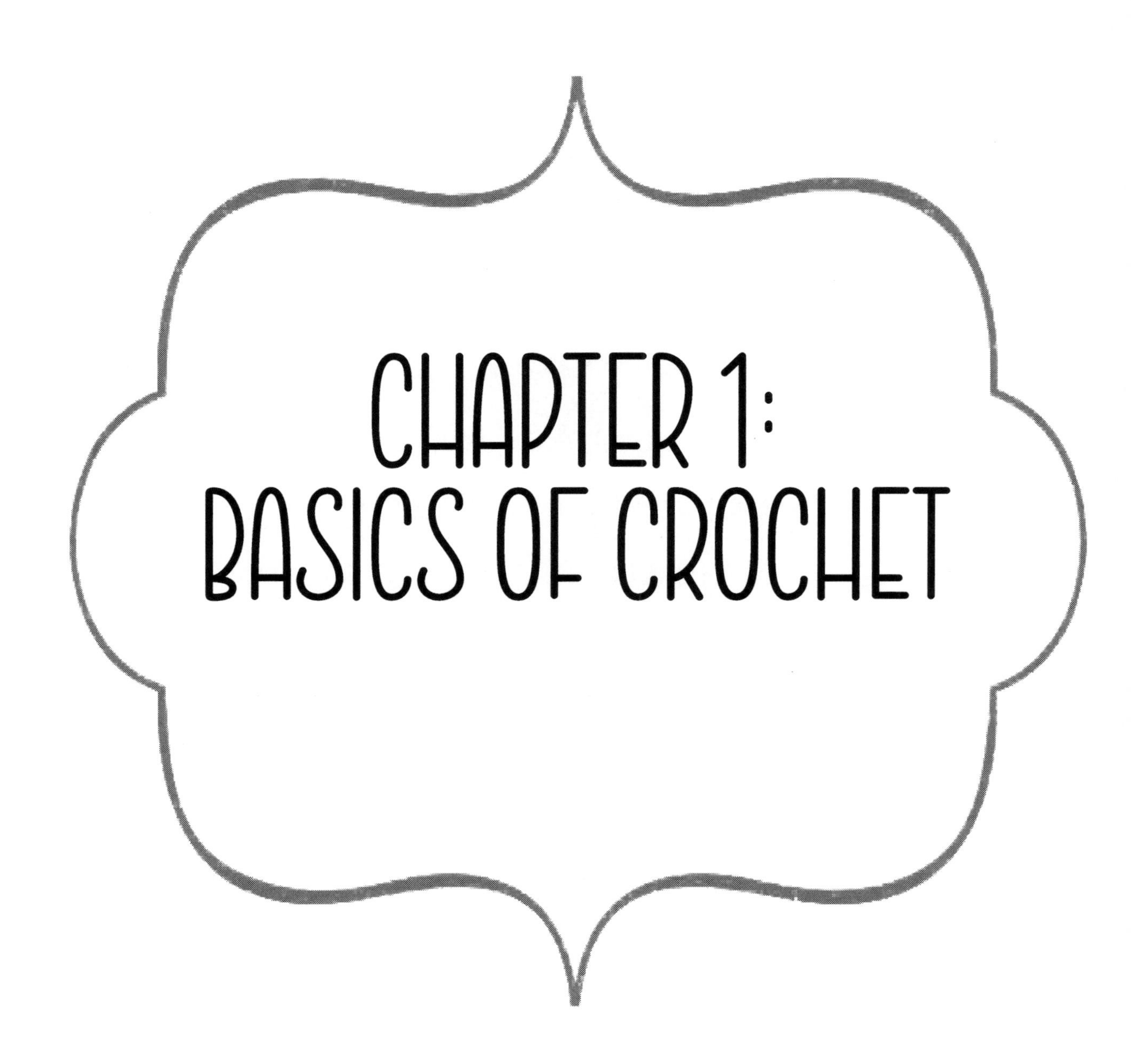

CHAPTER 1: BASICS OF CROCHET

Crochet is a needlework method that involves using a crochet hook and fiber or any mparable material to make a project. This material is most often crochet thread or yarn, t it could also be wire, fabric, twine, or other material.

rochet lovers want to finish crochet projects, which are usually useful, appealing, or help- in some manner. Afghans, baby booties, baby blankets, tote bags, scarves, granny uares, shawls, handbags, caps, and other popular items. Crochet may be used to make rious items, including socks, jewelry, and curtains.

s also feasible to crochet a variety of components for use in other projects. Crochet trim- ings and edgings, for example, are popular tasks that may be used on crocheted, knitted, d sewed objects (including ready-made items.) You might, for example, purchase some cks, towels, and pillows and crochet an edge on each.

ORIGIN OF CROCHETING

Crochet is a textile processing technique that has been valued and used on historical a tifacts since the 1800s. Crocheting is a method that involves using a crochet hook and matched yarn to make patterns that produce various structures and forms using variou stitches and techniques. Crocheting was originally used largely for constructing nets.

Crocheting employs a single crochet hook rather than two pointed needles, as seen to be the case with knitting. However, unlike knitting needles, this one has a hook at th end, which is why the word "needle" might be deceptive. The yarn is picked up with thes hooks, and the crochet stitches are made with them.

Crochet may generate considerably tighter / stronger stitches than knitting, and that is wh crocheted clothing is often firmer/ studier. Softer, less substantial designs, on the oth hand, maybe crocheted using the appropriate stitches. Of course, there are addition things to consider, such as the stitches employed, the kind of yarn used, the size of th crochet hook used, and your unique crocheting technique (firm or loose).

This is also why you can easily make three-dimensional things like Amigurumi (small ar big crocheted figurines), baskets, and other home goods with solid crochet stitches th keep their form.

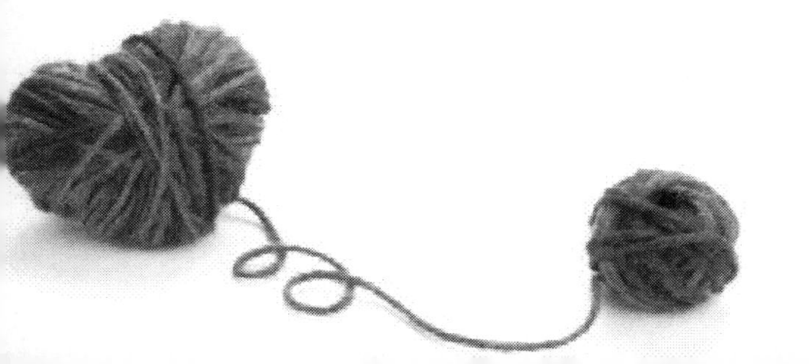

CROCHET VS. KNITTING

: first glance, beginners may find it difficult to distinguish between crocheting and knitting, ıt even though both involve yarn, there are several differences between the two crafts.

ıe tools employed are the first and most evident. Crocheters use a hook to grab onto the ırn, while knitters use two thin knitting needles. Crochet hooks are often constructed of uminum, plastic, bamboo, wood, or steel and are available in various sizes depending ı the material used.

rocheting uses just one hand, which some people find more convenient, and it is often ıicker than knitting. The end product is usually lighter and drapes better than knitted garents. Both crafts involve yarn, but Crochet is a little more forgiving. It's easy to crochet ıything with thread to the rope using various hook gauges.

titches are utilized in a variety of ways. Knitting mainly employs two stitches, but Crochet fers a vast array of complicated stitches to create various designs. Knitters have numerıs active loops on the needles at the same time. Therefore, the stitches generated vary idely. There is generally just one working loop at a time in Crochet. (Tunisian Crochet, hich employs extra-long needles to generate a knit-like output, is the exception to this le.)

ne connection is that both crafts employ abbreviated designs, many of which are the ame whether knitting or crocheting. It will be considerably simpler to switch between the arious crafts as a result of this. Of course, whether it's mittens, sweaters, blankets, or slipers, many of the products may be made in the same way. Both need patience and good and-eye coordination, so try them both and decide which you prefer.

ESSENTIAL CROCHET SUPPLIES

The essential tools you'll need to get started are a crochet hook and thread, yarn, or wi to make your material.

- **Crochet hooks** — Available in various gauges depending on the thickness of the ma terial to be looped, these metal or plastic tools come in various sizes.
- **Yarn and crochet threads** – Choosing your fibers is one of the most appealing par of crocheting. Again, the kind of yarn or thread you'll need will be determined by wh you're making.
- **Scissors** – Some of the favorite craft scissors are made by Fiskars.
- **Stitch markers** – These little locket-shaped parts will help you stay on track with you designs.

There are many different crochet stitches, but most crafts need to know how to form a sl knot to get the yarn on the hook and the chain stitch to make a solid row to anchor th whole work.

TYPES OF CROCHET

rochet comes in a variety of styles, similar to embroidery and quilting. These styles, which ere evolved according to local traditions in many countries, may have a wide range of im-acts. These techniques demonstrate the flexibility of the Crochet as an art form, whether enerating delicate lace or large weaved baskets. Depending on the ultimate result you esire, here are a few techniques you may want to consider.

- **Amigurumi:** This Japanese crochet technique is used to make little stuffed yarn animals. They're very popular because of their adorable look, and they're usually made using simple crochet stitches. To achieve a tight weave, smaller gauge crochet hooks are used.
- **Aran:** Aran is a textured yarn that is often used for bulky sweaters and blankets. It's a Celtic technique that involves several interwoven crochet cables and is also termed cable crochet. Aran is also named for moderately weight yarn that is more frequently known in the United States as worsted yarn. Don't be confused: Aran crochet does not need the usage of Aran yarn.
- **Bavarian:** Bavarian Crochet is the intermediate method that is often used to construct blankets and shawls. It is typically done in rounds rather than rows. The end product is a thick cloth with delicate color gradations.
- **Bosnian:** Frequently mistaken for knitting, Bosnian Crochet, usually called Shepherd's knitting, is made entirely of the slip stitch. While a conventional crochet hook may be used, some people prefer to use Bosnian crochet hooks since they are simpler to work with. Because the procedure is time-consuming, it is best used to make smaller items.
- **Clothesline:** This African and Nepalese method includes utilizing thick rope or chain to produce a strong, durable fabric often used to make baskets, bags, and carpets

- **Jiffy lace:** This traditional 19th-century method is also known as broomstick lac A hook and a long wooden dowel are used. "The pattern is formed by pulling lor loops of the thread up onto the dowel (traditionally, a broomstick, that is where tl term derives from)," according to Red Heart.
- **Cro-Hook:** A cro-hook is a double-sided hook used in this Tunisian crochet styl This lets you produce double-sided cloth by working in two colors at the same tim Cro-knit, double-ended Tunisian, and double hook crochet are all terms for the sam method, ideal for making multicolored scarves and blankets.
- **Irish lace:** This method, also known as Irish lace, requires using extremely fine cr chet hooks and linen or cotton thread. Its usage dates back to the nineteenth centu when the Irish created it to replicate more costly Venetian lace. After the Irish Pota Famine, the skill was utilized to boost the economy, and by the mid-nineteenth ce tury, about 12,000 Irish women were crocheting.
- **Tapestry:** A beautiful method for making colorful and patterned textiles, tapestry cr chet employs a variety of colored yarns to create a fabric that seems nearly wove rather than crocheted. Similar methods are known as intarsia, colorwork, jacquar and mosaic Crochet. Tapestry crochet is widely used by the native Wayuu people Venezuela and Colombia to construct little purses known as mochila. In Guatema and Africa, it is used to produce hats.
- **Tunisian:** Tunisian Crochet is a common method that involves using a crochet hoc that is exceptionally long and has a stopper at the end. It's also known as Afgha crochet, and it's similar to knitting as it involves working numerous loops at onc The method creates a noticeably thick fabric and less malleable fabric than oth crochet styles, making it ideal for blankets and winter caps rather than the soft wearable goods.

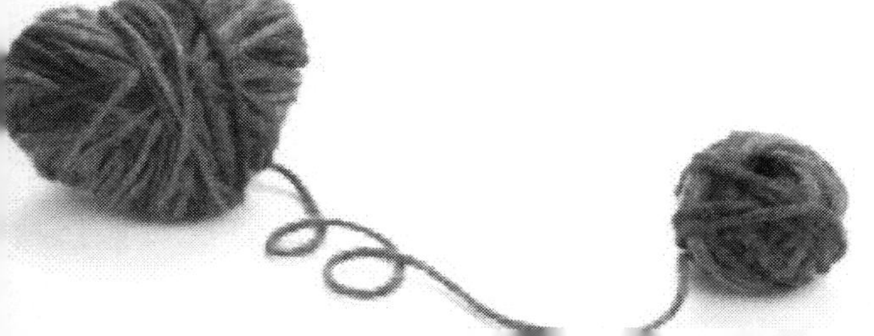

HOW TO READ A CROCHET?

eading crochet designs may be somewhat intimidating for novices with all those numbers nd letters that appear like hieroglyphics. It's a lot simpler to interpret your pattern if you nderstand how to split it down. These are some pointers to get you started; keep them in ind, and you'll be able to read patterns like a pro in no time.

1. Choosing a Crochet Pattern

ormally, while choosing a pattern, you would just look for a design you like and begin ewing. If you're a newbie, though, a project with a tutorial is preferable to a text-based esign.

ou should also consider the four crochet skill levels: beginner, easy, intermediate, and adanced/experienced. Beginners should start with a beginning design, which only requires ndamental stitches and minimum shaping methods, before progressing to easy patterns, hich demand a broader set of abilities.

2. Reading a Crochet Pattern

nce you've decided on a pattern, settle down and go through it again to make sure you asp all the project requirements. The following parts are found in most crochet patterns:

- Yarn, supplies, and notions required
- An "about" section with pattern notes (if available)
- Abbreviations used
- Any unique stitches used
- Information on gauge, tension, or size

ey all give helpful (and sometimes critical) information that you should know before you egin. Let's take a closer look at them.

- **The About Section**

Pay attention to which crochet terms are used in this section, as there are internatio al differences between terms used in the U.S. and the U.K. You want your pattern to written in the terminology you're used to.

- **Yarn, Materials and Notions**

Double-check you have all the yarn and materials you need. If you're using multip skeins of yarn with different dye lot numbers, you should know how to manipula them to avoid awkward and unintentional color variations.

- **Gauge and Tension**

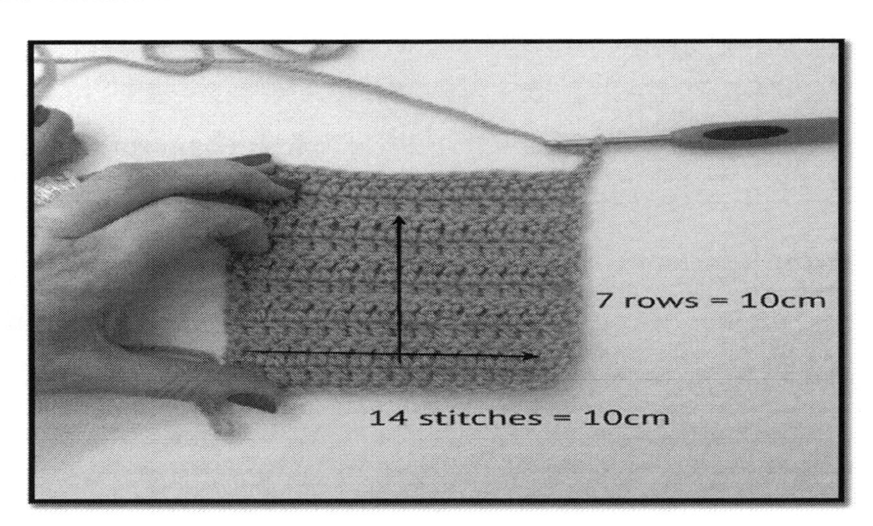

Always create a gauge swatch before starting your item unless it's a scarf or blanket. Th gauge may seem like unnecessary effort (particularly if you're eager to get started), but guarantees that your project is a perfect size. Typically, a design will state: 14 stitches = 10 cm (4″); 7 rows = 10 cm (4″) in double crochet with a size G hook (4mm) Let's break down: You'll need the G hook and yarn you plan to use for the project to produce a gaug swatch.

fter making the first chain, make a few extra chains than the number specified in the pat-rn. The design calls for 14 stitches in this instance, so create roughly 20. To complete e swatch, stitch at least Ten rows of double Crochet. Now it's time to double-check your auge.

rst, use a ruler to determine how many stitches will fit into a 4″ square (you must have 4). Then see how many rows you can fit into a 4″ square (this must be 7). You have the ght gauge if your numbers are accurate. There are two techniques to correct a misaligned auge. If you have more rows and stitches than the gauge asks for, go up a hook size or alf a size. This will allow you to crochet more loosely to get the desired gauge. Go down e hook size / half a size if you have fewer stitches and rows than required.

- **Symbols:**

In a pattern row, an asterisk or a dagger indicates that a section of the instructions will e repeated. "Rep from * 3 times," for example, indicates that even after working the in-ructions once, you have to work them three more times for a total of four times. ** "Rep om * across, ending last rep at **," may employ double asterisks to indicate a spot in e instructions where a repetition should be stopped before it is finished. ( ) Instructions cluded in parentheses must be completed the number of times stated after the parenthe-s. For example, "(ch 1, sc, ch 1) 3 times" indicates chain 1, single crochet, then chain 1 ree times again for the total of the 6 chains & 3 single crochets. Parentheses may also e used to separate or define a group of stitches that will be worked together in the same ea or thread. "(dc, ch 2, dc) in corner sp,". [] [] Additional information is also provided by ackets & ( ) parentheses.

Abbreviations Used

Reading crochet designs is just like reading a foreign language with a lot of acronyms. It may be difficult at first, but shorthand will quickly become second nature. It's a good idea to familiarize yourself with the crochet stitch dictionary, but here's a quick rundown of acronyms that novices are likely to encounter:

- **ch** = chain stitch
- **beg** = beginning
- **dec** = decrease
- **ch-sp** = chain space
- **inc** = increase
- **dc** = double Crochet
- **mc** = main color
- **rs** = right side
- **rep** = repeat
- **sl st** = slip Stitch
- **sc** = single Crochet
- **tr** = treble Crochet
- **st** = stitch
- **ws** = wrong side
- YO =Yarn over

It's worth noting that some designers use somewhat different terminology when describing patterns. To signify creating four foundation chains, one would write "4ch," while another might write "Ch 4." Despite these minor variations, the pattern must be simple to follow if you know the abbreviations.

- **Special Stitches Used**

onfirm the pattern instructions and practice it on some spare yarn if the pattern has a itch, you've never done before. If you're having trouble executing the new technique, ok for a tutorial to practice with until you're comfortable with it.

3. **Decoding a Pattern**

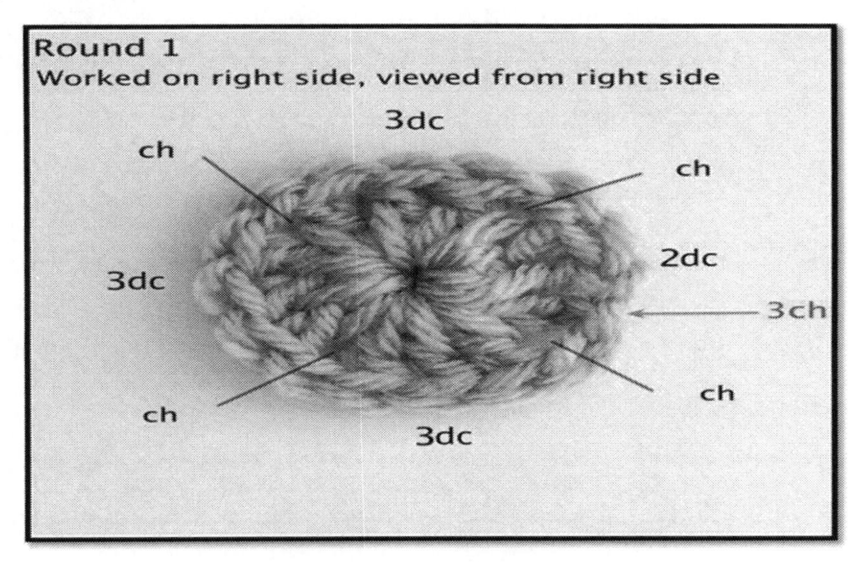

et's stroll through a basic granny square so you may decode the pattern language now hat you know what to anticipate from each component of a design. It will resemble the ollowing:

ound One (RS): Begin by yarn A. To make a ring, link 4ch with sl st. 3 ch (counts as a c). Then 2dc into a ring, then into 1 ch. * 3dc into ring, 1ch* rep two more times. To join, l st. Finish by fastening off the yarn A.

The following is a breakdown of the line:

1. Work on the right side for this round (RS).
2. Create a foundation chain with four chains using yarn A (your first yarn color), the slip stitch in the first chain to create a ring.
3. Chain three times to make the double crochet stitch.
4. In the ring, add two additional double crochet stitches. After that, construct a chair
5. *Insert three additional double crochet stitches into a ring, then chain. Repeat th final two steps (the ones marked with asterisks) twice more.
6. Tie a knot on your yarn.

Now for the **second round**:

Round 2: Switch to the WS and work on it. 3ch, join yarn B into any ch sp; 3ch. 1dc, 1c For next ch sp; 3dc, 2ch, 3dc, 1ch. * Repeat two more times. 3 dc, 2 ch, 1 dc in first spac sl st to connect, yarn B fastened off.

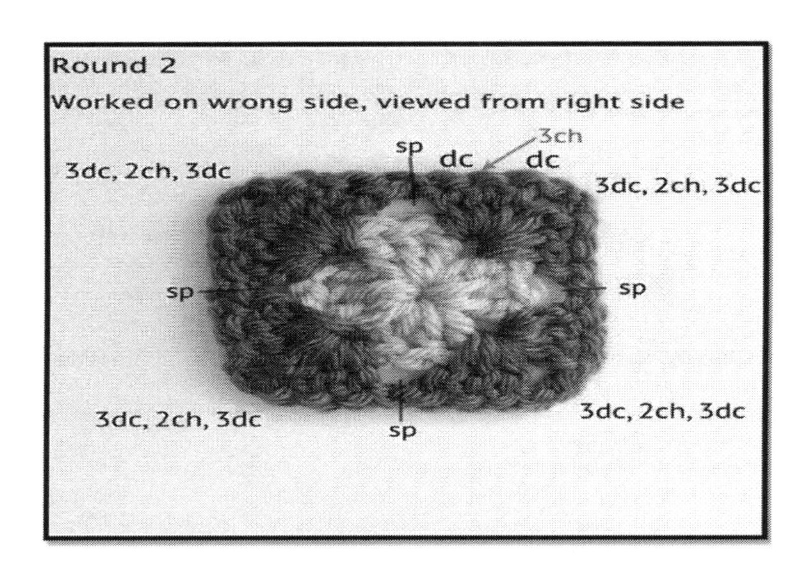

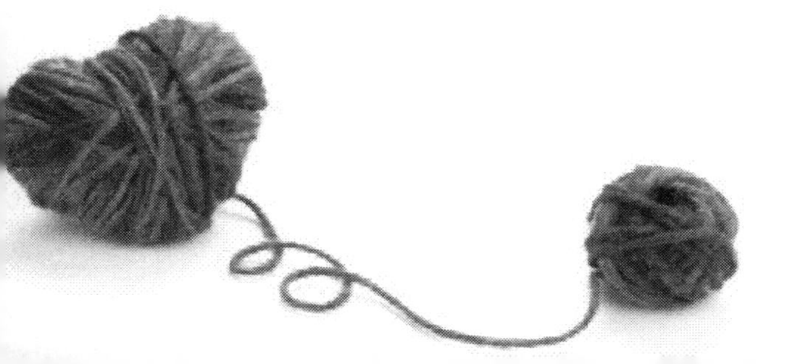

Turn the work over so that you're working on the wrong side of Round 2.

Insert your second color of yarn into any of the chain spaces. 3 chains, 1 double crochet itch, and 1 chain are made.

*Work on 3 double crochet stitches, 2 chains, 3 additional double crochet stitches, and chain on the next chain gap. In each of the following two chain gaps, repeat the previous ep (steps between the asterisks).

To finish the first corner, work on 3 double crochet stitches, 2 chains, and 1 double cro-
het stitch when you reach the first chain gap.

Slip Stitch into the top of your three beginning chains to finish the circle. Finish by tying f your yarn.

hen go on to round three:

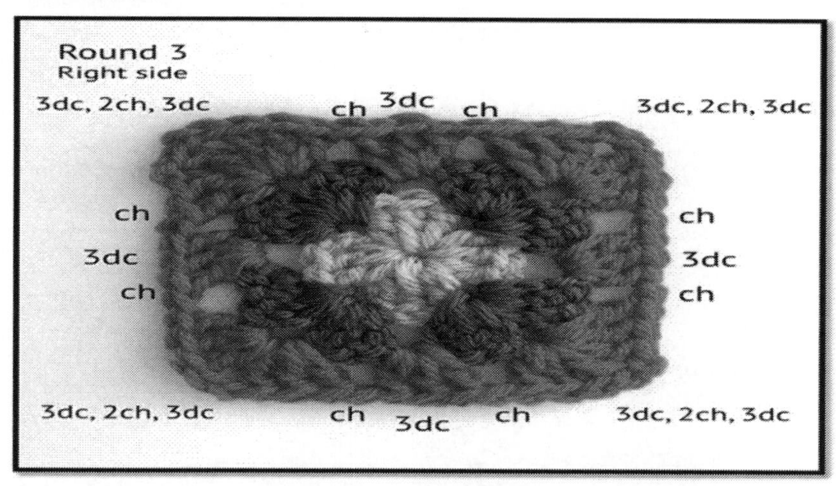

ound 3: Begin working on RS. Any corner area may be linked with yarn C. 3ch, 1 dc, 1ch. hen *3dc into the ch sp 1 ch 3dc 2ch 3dc, ch into the next corner sp. Then * Rep it from to * two more times. 3dc, into the ch sp 1ch and 3dc 2ch 1dc into the first corner sp, To in, sl st. Finish by fastening off the yarn C.

1.1 Reverse your work so that you're working on the right side.

1.2 In any corner spot, join your third color of yarn.

1.3 Chain three times, double Crochet once, then chain one more.

1.4 *Make three double crochets in the next chain gap, then one chain. Work c 3 double crochets, 2 chains and 3 double crochets following the chain. * Two time over, repeat the instructions between the asterisks.

1.5 Make 3 double crochets into the next chain space to finish the last side. 1 Chain

1.6 Make 3 double crochets, two chains, and 1 more double crochet to finish th corner. With a slip stitch, join the circle to the top of the beginning chains. Finish b tying off your yarn.

Round 4: Switch to WS and work on it. Link Yarn D with any corner sp 3ch 1dc 1ch The *3dc 1ch in the following two ch sps. 3dc, 2ch, 3dc, with next corner sp. Rep it from * to two more times. 3dc, 1ch into next 2 ch sp 3dc 2ch 1dc into first corner sp, Join with a st and fasten off.

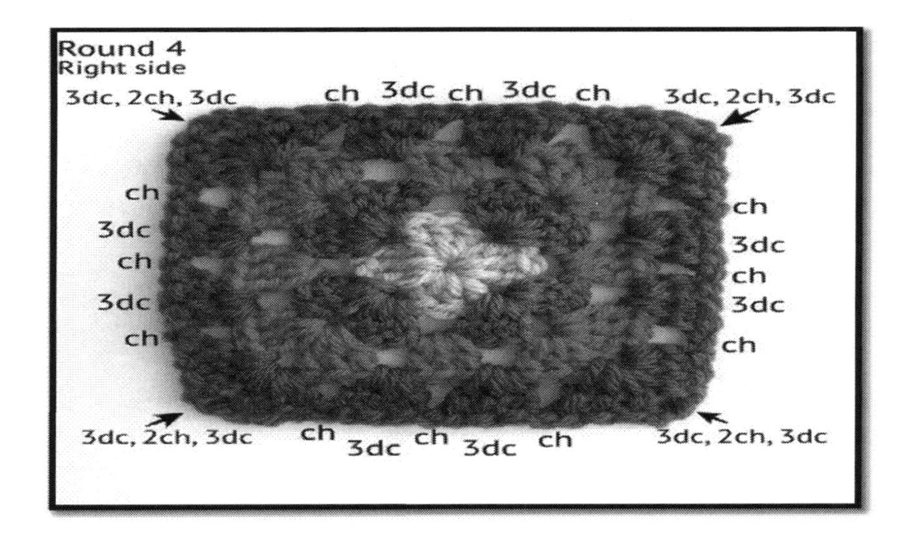

ound 5: Switch to the right side and work on the RS. Link Yarn E to any corner sp 3ch :h 1dc, Then *3dc and 1ch into 3 ch sps. *Rep it from the * to ** for twice more. Then lc, 1 ch into the 3 ch sp 3dc 1dc2ch into a first corner sp Join with a sl st and fasten off.

fter you've learned the pattern language, it a time to start working on your first project.

TIPS FOR CROCHET BEGINNERS

It’s never simple to learn a new skill. You’ve come to the right place if you’ve decided it time to learn to Crochet. These books offer everything you’ll need to start (hooks, pattern yarn, and tips from the experts). Here are some crochet suggestions for beginners:

1. Keep your stitches flexible and relaxed.

When you’re learning anything new, it’s normal to feel nervous. The more intricate th Stitch, the more tightly you will grasp your hook. Refrain from doing so, take a deep breat and keep the stitches slack and relaxed. The looser the stitches are, the simpler it will b to enter your hook and complete the project!

2. Practice.

Before you begin, read over the pattern you want to create. If you notice a stitch, you’v never attempted before (like single Crochet, shell stitches, double Crochet), take yo hook and yarn and practice them before beginning your project. By the time you get to th Stitch in the design, you’ll be completely confident in your ability to execute it.

Most designs call for a “gauge swatch,” which is often a square sample measuring 4” x 4 While producing the gauge swatch, practice your new stitches to improve your techniqu and ensure that you are knitting the product to the right size.

3. Experiment using various tools.

If you’re new to start crocheting, it’s a good idea to buy a couple of different hooks to e periment with. You could need a hook with the deeper bowl/ mouth if you’re having troub catching the loop on your hook. If you’re having trouble placing your hook into the Stitc you may need a hook with the pointier head. A new hook might be the difference betwee success and failure.

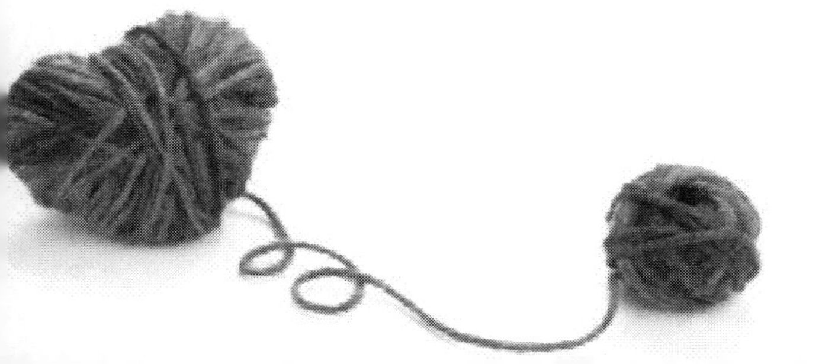

Experiment with various yarns.

eginners should choose worsted weight yarn that is smooth and doesn't split easily (Bra- Worsted is recommended). However, everyone has their preferences. Feel free to ex- eriment with various yarns.

Understand the concept of gauge.

his is a frequent beginner error to avoid. It's all about the Gauge! Gauge is a measure- ent that informs you how many rows and stitches your crochet pattern should fit into a ertain number of inches. This should be included in every pattern. If you want your com- eted creation to look like the photographs or fit in a certain size, you'll need to match your auge to the pattern's specifications. Many people miss this stage and wind up with a big ough hat as a chair cover. Try to learn about gauge early; it'll pay later!

To frog or not to frog that is the question!

hat exactly is frogging? It's when you "rip it." If you pay close attention to detail and no- ce a mistake the few rows back, it's worth frogging back and correcting the error (it will ug you forever). If the error isn't obvious, consider if you want to go back and correct it. verybody has different choices. Don't feel bad about your decision.

Don't put too much pressure on yourself.

istakes are bound to occur. Even the most skilled and meticulous crocheters make errors om time to time. There is no such thing as a flawless first project (first 10 projects). Don't e too hard on yourself if you make a mistake. Be proud of what you've learned and know at you'll become better with practice.

CHAPTER 2: BASIC CROCHET STITCHES

Crochet is a simple craft to learn. For making a broad range of items, you need to aster a few stitches. This chapter includes information on the six most basic beginning ochet stitches.

ou'll be able to produce a crochet slip and chain stitch in no time, allowing you to begin mple crafts. Learn additional basic stitches after that and start making scarves, caps, awls, and blankets.

CROCHET CHAIN STITCH

Learn the slip knot before moving on to the chain stitch since it's what you'll need to ho the yarn on the hook to start crocheting. Then master the fundamental chain stitch, whi is abbreviated as "ch" in designs. Most crochet projects start with a collection of cha stitches known as a base chain, beginning chain, or foundation chain.

In a crochet project, a turning chain is often used to begin each new row. The turnir chain's height, or the number of chains you make, is determined by the stitches used that row. A triple crochet row, for example, starts with three chains.

Crochet chains, especially when working in the round, are often used to link other stitch in the crochet design. A "ch 2" separates the double crochet stitches in the basic croch granny square pattern, for example, to create a gap in each corner of the square.

The picot stitch is typical Crochet edging with a texture created by a crochet chain. Croch chains are a common design element in lengthy fringe, openwork lace/ mesh, and hu loops.

Experiment with a basic crochet chain in a small project. Make your first basic crochet sca by crocheting a series of long chains and knotting them together at both ends.

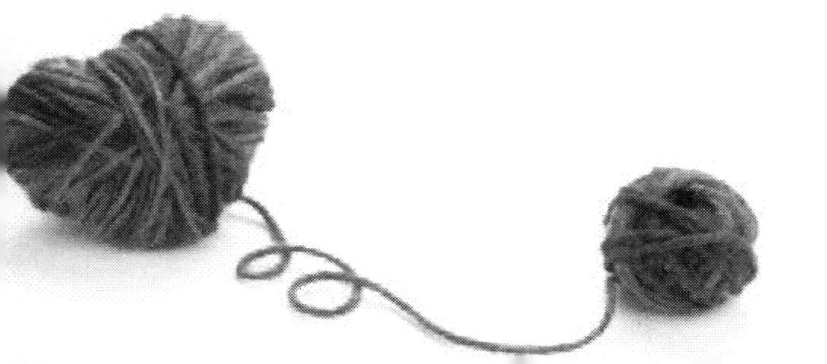

CROCHET SLIP STITCH

ip stitches in Crochet are simple and small. All Crochet is built on top of these. In a pattrn, slip stitch is commonly abbreviated as "sl st." When knitting in the round, the slip stitch most often used when you're told to "connect with a slip stitch to make a ring" /"slip stitch finish round."

ip stitches may be used to connect two crocheted elements. Slip Stitch crochet the gran- squares together that are paced side by side.

rochet slip stitches are often used to give flourishes to projects. Slip stitches, for exame, offer color and aesthetic interest to the surface of the crochet or knitting product in the ırface crochet. It's almost as if you're embroidering a flourish on a crocheted piece using ip stitches.

SINGLE CROCHET STITCH

ıe crochet slip and chain stitch provide a stable foundation for starting crochet projects. A ngle crochet stitch allows you to crochet a wider range of crafts. The single crochet stitch, ɔbreviated as "sc," is used in many designs. Single crochet stitches are small stitches at work together to produce a thick fabric. You can make varying thicknesses by using fferent sizes of hooks and yarn and changing the Stitch. You can adjust the single crochet itch based on which loops you work through. In all amigurumi crochet designs, the sine crochet stitch serves as the foundation stitch. Knitting or crocheting miniature stuffed ıimals and other three-dimensional things are known as amigurumi in Japan. Crocheting ves amigurumi products the perfect density of the fabric.

HALF DOUBLE CROCHET STITCH

The half-double crochet stitch adds a step to the basic single crochet stitch. Half doub crochet stitch has a height that is midway between single & double crochet stitch. Mar projects use the Stitch, which is abbreviated as "hdc."

The half-double crochet pattern is more open than a single crochet stitch, but it still pr vides adequate density for warm projects. The half-double crochet stitch is also faster tha the single crochet stitch in making fabric. When you need to crochet a piece quickly, th Stitch comes in handy.

DOUBLE CROCHET STITCH

The basic stitches work well with the double crochet stitch, abbreviated as "dc." Granr square Crochet, v-stitch Crochet, fillet crochet, and other popular crochet patterns use th double crochet stitch. The fundamental double Crochet is used in these designs to give a otherwise simple item a new aesthetic.

You can make the double crochet stitch look different depending on which loops you wo through after you've mastered it. Working in the back loop, for example, results in a ribbe pattern that looks great on blankets, cuffs, and hatbands.

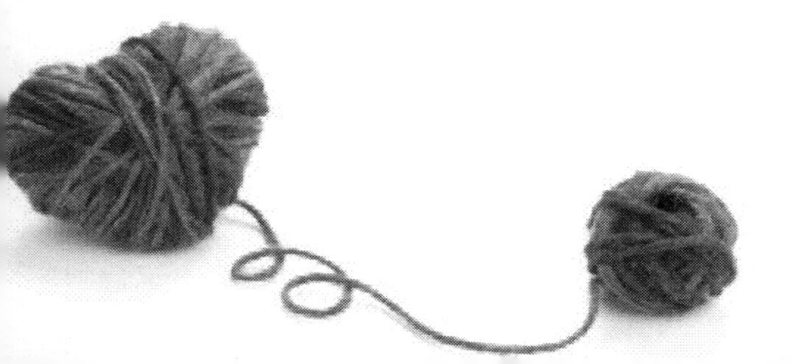

TREBLE CROCHET STITCH

crochet patterns, the treble crochet stitch (also known as triple crochet stitch) is abbre-ated as "tr." The Stitch is higher than the double crochet stitch and has the same funda-ental stages as the double crochet stitch.

ou can produce many taller crochet stitches after knowing how to double Crochet, includ-g the triple treble, double treble, and even taller stitches.

is Stitch may be used to increase the height of a project swiftly. Longer stitches result a looser fabric. Crochet fabric that is looser drapes better and breathes better, making it xcellent for lacy, open shawls and light blankets with higher stitches.

ou're well on your way towards becoming an expert crocheter now that you've learned ese six fundamental crochet stitches. Experiment with different stitch patterns by mixing e basic crochet stitches. The crochet seed stitch, for example, alternates single and dou-e crochet stitches, whereas the crochet moss stitch contrasts single and double crochet itches.

MORE CROCHET STITCHES TO LEARN

ventually, you'll be able to create a more advanced crochet stitch like a bubble stitch, ell stitch, Ripple stitch, or even crochet cables using the fundamental crochet stitches.

ere are a few stunning stitches, although it is by no means exhaustive. With a skein of rn & your trusty crochet hook, the world is your oyster!

- **Bubbles**

Chain multiple: 3 + 2

Stitch Guide

(YO, insert a hook in appropriate s YO and draw up a lp to a height of dc, YO and draw through the 2 lps c a hook) 5 times, YO & draw throug the 6 lps on a hook: CL created.

Instructions

Row 1: Work Sc in the 2nd ch from a hook & in each rem ch; ch 1 and turn

Row 2 (RS): Work Sc in first sc; *CL in the next sc, sc in the next 2 sc; rep fro the * across; ch 1, turn.

Row 3: Work Sc in an each st, across; work ch 1, turn.

Row 4: Work Sc in the first 2 sc, Work CL in next sc; *sc in next 2 sc, work CL in next sc; the rep from * across, work sc in the last sc; ch 1 and turn.

Row 5: Sc in the each st across; work ch 1, turn. Rep from rows 2–5 for the pattern.

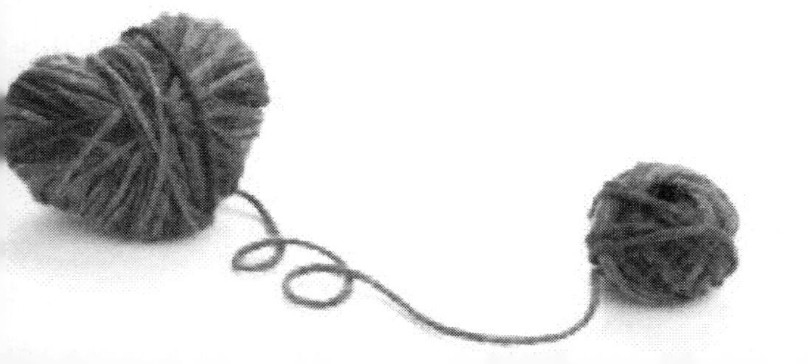

➢ **Baby Bobbles**

Chain multiple: 2 + 1

Instructions

Work all; sl sts loosely.

Row 1: Work Sl st in the 3rd ch from a hook; *hdc in the next ch, work sl st in the next ch; rep from the * across; work ch 2, turn.

Row 2 (RS): work Sk first sl st; work l st in the next hdc, work hdc in the next sl st; the rep from * across, sl st in top of turning ; ch 2, turn.

ep the row 2 for the pattern.

- **Bobblin' Along**

Chain multiple: 4 + 3

Stitch Guide

Bobble (BB): Yarn over insert hoc in defined st & draw up a lp to th height of a dc, YO then draw through 2 lps; (YO, then inse hook in the same st & draw up a lp, then YO & draw through the lps) 4 times, YO & draw throug all 6 lps on a hook; ch 1: BB mad

Instructions

Row 1 (RS): Work Dc in the 4th ch from a hook & in each rem ch; in ch 1, turn.

Row 2: work Sc in each of the first 2 sts; Work *BB in the next st, work sc in each of th next 3 sts; then rep from the * to the last 3 sts, work BB in the next st, work sc in each the last 2 sts; work ch 3, turn.

Row 3: work Dc in and each st across, work sk turning the ch; ch 1 and turn.

Row 4: work Sc in each of the first 4 sts; work *BB in the next st, work sc in each of next 3 st then rep from the * across, then ending with the sc in a top of the turning ch; in ch 3, tur

Row 5: Then-Rep row 3. Then-Rep rows 2–5 for the patt.

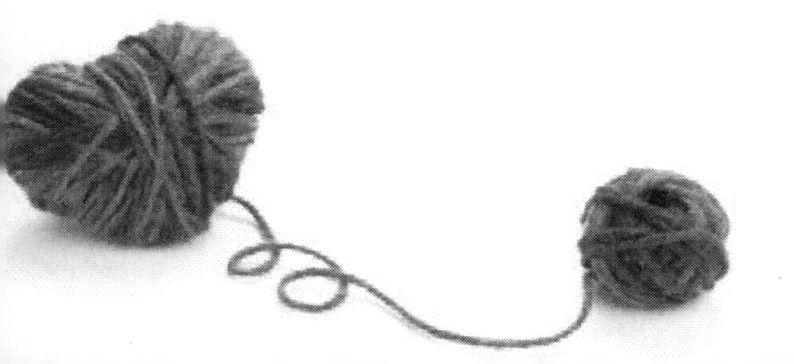

➢ **Fancy Floral**

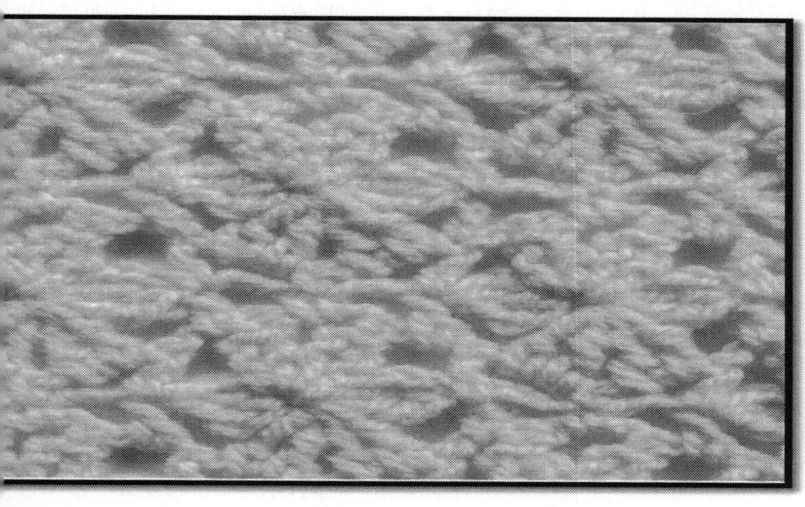

Chain multiple: 10 + 2

Stitch Guide Bobble (BB): Do *YO twice, put a hook in designated st or sp & draw up an lp, (YO & draw through two lps on hook) twice; rep from * one more in the same st / sp; YO and draw through all three lps on the hook: BB formed.

hell: Work (BB, ch 3, BB) in the specified ch/ st: shell made.

obble cluster (BBCL): *YO two times, insert a hook in top of the last dc (or 3rd ch of rning ch-6) and draw up an lp, (YO & draw through Two lps on a hook) two times; rep om the * once in the top of same dc (or in the same ch); **YO twice, insert a hook in next ı-sp and draw up an lp, (YO & draw through two lps on hook) twice; rep from ** once the same ch-sp***; then rep from the ** to *** once in the next ch-sp; then YO & draw rough the all 7 lps on a hook, ch 1: BBCL is made.

structions

ow 1: Work on shell in the 7th ch from a hook; then *ch 2, then sk next two chs, then dc in the ext ch, in ch 3, sk next two chs, sc in the next ch, work on ch 3, work on sk next two chs, ork on dc in the next ch, work on ch 2, work on sk for next 2 chs, work on shell in the next ı; then rep from the * across to the last 3 chs, sk the next 2 chs, dc in the last ch; work ı 6 (counts as dc & ch-3, sp throughout), then turn.

Row 2: Work *Sc in the next ch-sp, then in ch 3**; dc in the next ch-sp, in ch 3, work c BBCL, in ch 3, BB in the top of the last BBCL, then dc in the next ch-sp, ch 3; then rep fro the * across, ending in final rep at **; work sk next BB, dc in the next ch; ch 6, then turn.

Row 3: *Sc in the next sc, then ch 3**; dc in the next dc, ch 2, work on shell in th top of next BBCL, for ch 2, dc in the next dc, ch 3; rep from the * across, ending in the fin rep at **; dc in the 3rd ch of turning of ch-6; ch 6, turn.

Row 4: *Work on BBCL, in ch 3, BB in the top of a last BBCL**; work on dc in the next c sp, in ch 3, sc in the next ch-sp, in ch 3, dc in the next ch-sp, in ch 3; rep from the * acros ending the final rep at **; dc in the 3rd ch of turning ch-6; in ch 3 (counts as dc of the ne row), then turn.

Row 5: *Work on shell in the top of the next BBCL**; ch 2, dc in the next dc, ch 3, sc in th next sc, ch 3, dc in the next dc, in ch 2; rep from the * across, ending the final rep at **; d in the 3rd ch of turning ch-6; in ch 6, turn. Then-Rep rows 2–5 for the patt.

➢ **Shell Ripple**

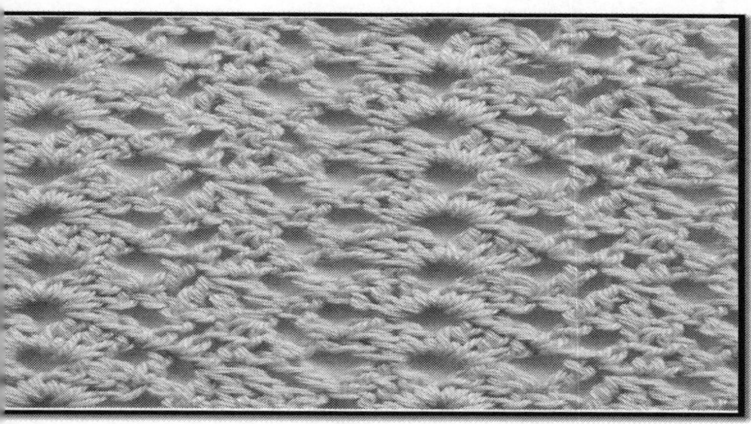

Chain multiple: 11 + 3

Stitch Guide Cluster (CL): CL was created by keeping the final lp of each dc on the hook and dc in the specified 3 sts, YO, and drawing through all of 4 lps on hook.

Shell: (3 dc, ch 3, 3 dc) in the specified st / sp.

structions

ow 1 (RS): Dc in the 3rd ch from a hook, ch 1, sk next ch, dc in the next ch; ch 1, sk the ext ch, 3 dc in the next ch; ch 3, 3 dc in the next ch; ch 1, sk in next ch, dc in the next ch, 1 1; *sk the next ch, CL over the next 3 chs; ch 1, sk the next ch, dc in the next ch, ch 1; sk e next ch, 3 dc in the next ch; ch 3, 3 dc in the next ch, ch 1, sk the next ch, dc in the next 1, ch 1; rep from the * to last four chs; (sk the next ch, dc in the next ch) twice; ch 2, turn.

ow 2: Sk the first 2 dc, (dc in the next dc, in ch 1) twice; sk the next 2 dc, shell in the ext ch-3 sp; ch 1, work sk in next 2 dc, dc in the next dc, ch 1; *CL over the next dc, next L & next dc; ch 1, dc in the next dc, ch 1, sk the next 2 dc; shell in the next ch-3 sp; ch 1, the next 2 dc, dc in the next dc, ch 1; rep from the * to last 2 dc; dc in the last 2 dc; ch turn.

ow 3: Sk the first 2 dc, (dc in the next dc, ch 1) twice; sk the next 2 dc, shell in the ext ch-3 sp, work ch 1, sk the next 2 dc, dc in the next dc, in ch 1; *CL over the next dc, ext CL, & next dc; ch 1, dc in the next dc, ch 1, sk the next 2 dc, shell in the next ch-3 sp; 1 1, sk the next 2 dc, dc in the next dc, in ch 1; rep from the * to the last 2 dc; dc in the last dc; in ch 2, turn, leaving the turning ch unworked.

hen-Rep row 3 for the patt.

- **Textured Ripple**

Chain multiple: 9 + 3

Two colors: color A & color B

Instructions

Work beg the ch with a color A.

Row 1 (WS): Work Sc in the 2nd ch from a hook and in the next 4 chs, 3 sc in next ch; th n *sc in the next 3 chs, then sk in next 2 chs, then sc in the next 3 chs, 3 sc in the next c then rep from the * across to the last 5 chs, the sc in the last 5 chs; in ch 1, turn.

Row 2 (RS): Working only in the back lps, dec over the first 2 sts (to work in dec: draw up lp an each of two sts indicated, YO & draw through the all 3 lps on a hook: dec is made); s in the next 4 sc, then 3 sc in the next sc; *sc in the next 3 sc, sk the next 2 sc, sc in the ne 3 sc, 3 sc in the next sc; rep from the * to last 6 sc, sc in the next 4 sc, dec over the last sc; ch 1, then turn.

Rows 3-5: Then-Rep row 2. At the end of row 5, do not ch 1. Then Finish off color A.

Row 6: With the right side facing you & color B, working through both lps, work sl st loose in each sc across. Then Finish off color B.

Row 7: With the wrong side facing you & color A, leaving the sl sts of the prev row u worked & working in the back lps only of the sc of row 5, then rep row 2. Then-Rep row 2–7 for the patt.

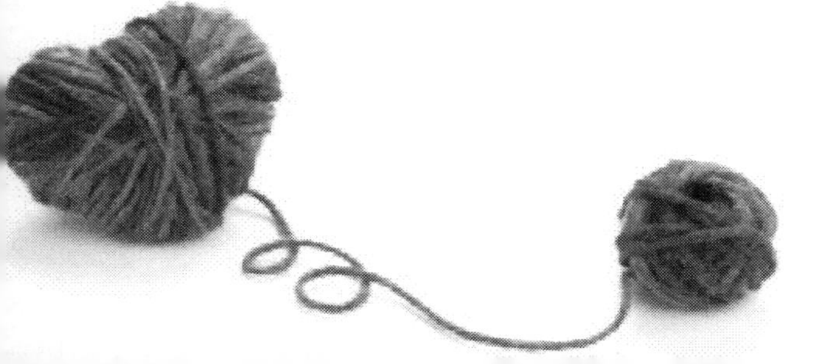

CHAPTER 3: CROCHET TECHNIQUES

This section starts with the fundamentals of crochet techniques. If you're a beginner crocheter, some of the illustrated instructions are a terrific place to start with.

HOLDING THE HOOK

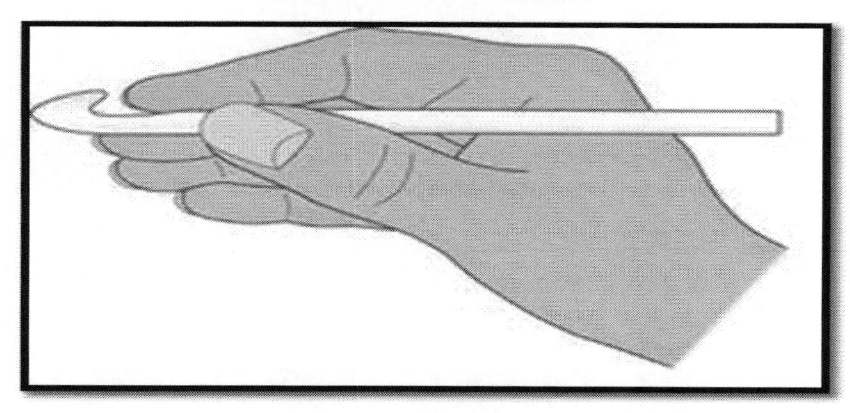

Pen Position: As though you pick up a pencil or pen, pick up your hook. Then turn your hand while the palm is facing up, whereas the hook is balanced in your hand and laying in the gap between your index finger and thumb while holding the hook loosely between your fingers and thumb.

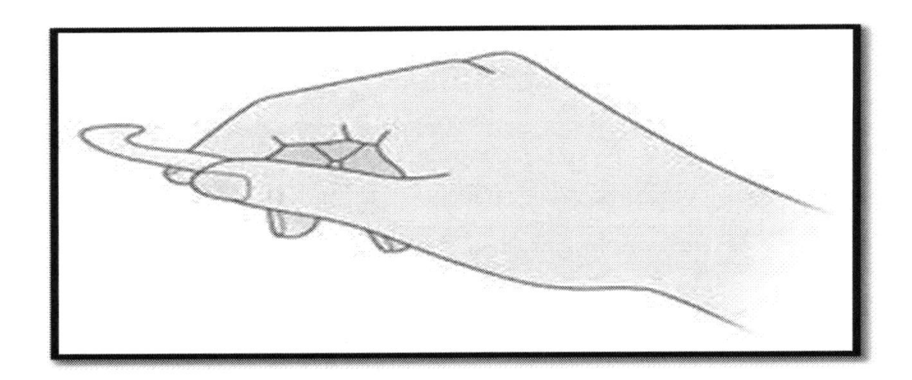

Knife Position: You can switch to a knife position if you work with a big hook and thi yarn. As being overly tensed might harm your arm or shoulder while crocheting. Make su you constantly take breaks and are comfortable.

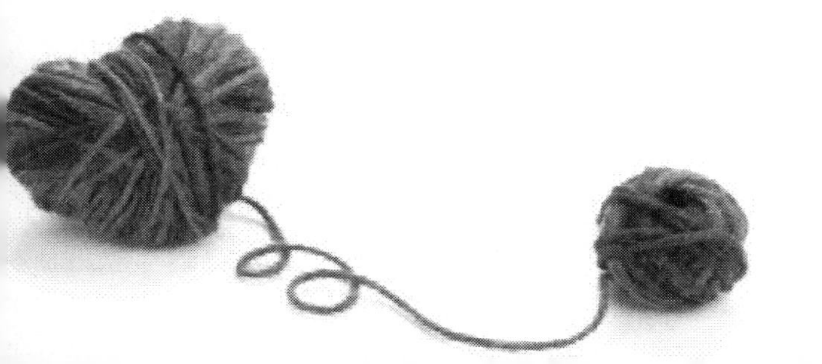

HOLDING THE YARN

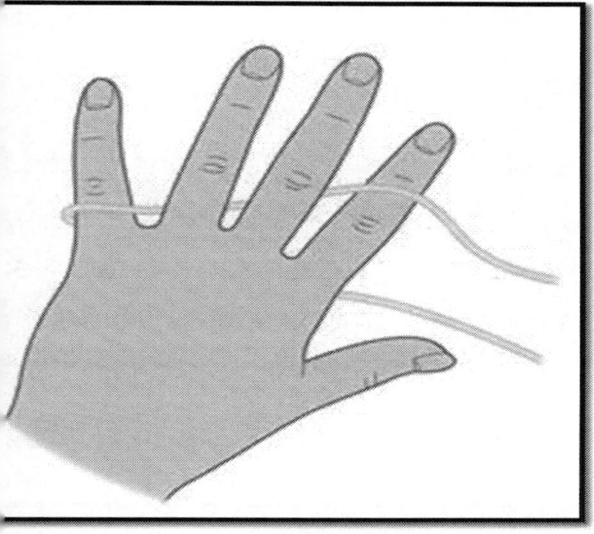

With your palm facing upwards and the short end in front, pick up your yarn with the little finger in the opposite hand to your hook. Turn your hand so that the yarn is on top of your index finger and beneath the other two fingers and wrapped right around your little finger, as seen above.

urn your hand to face you, your thumb nd middle finger poised to take up the task. sing the same hand, hold the work or the slip not between your middle finger and thumb, ght below the crochet hook & loop/s on the ook, with your index finger curled slightly.

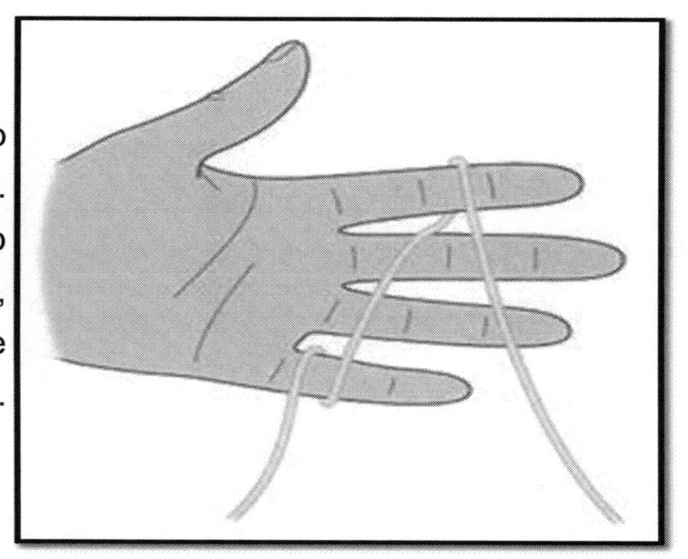

HOLDING YOUR HOOK, YARN, AND CROCHET

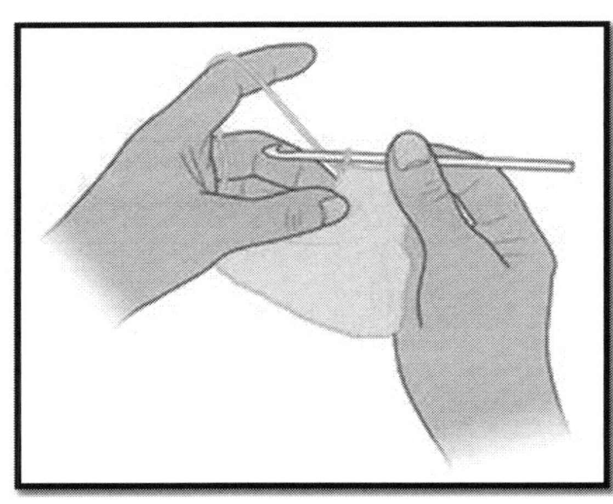

➢ **Yarn round hook**

Maintain a slight bend in your index fing with the yarn draped over it and hold the wo (or slip knot) between your middle finger ar thumb, underneath the crochet hook, as well a the loop/s on the hook, using the same han

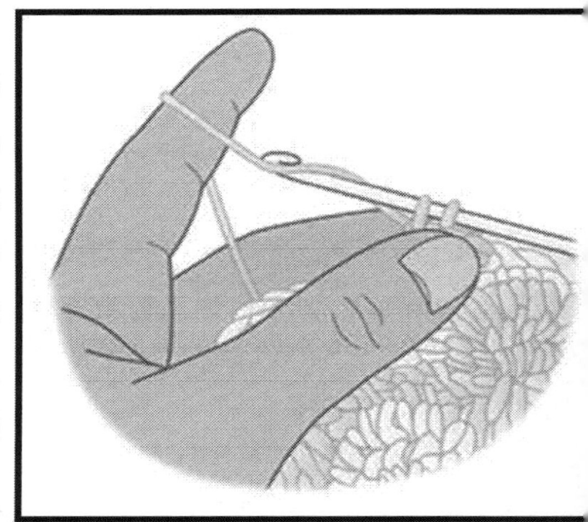

Loosen the yarn on your index finger as you pull the loop through the hook to keep the loop slack. The yarn will get too tight and drag the loop on a hook too tight for you to drag the yarn through if you tighten your index finger. Some left-handed people learn to crochet in the same way as right-handed people, while others learn with the hook in the left hand and yarn in the right.

Grab the yarn from behind with a hook pointed upwards to make a stitch. Turn the hoo so it faces downwards and slips the yarn through the loop while carefully pulling the ya through the loop on the hook. The loop on a hook should be maintained slack enough allow the hook to pass through easily.

Making a slip knot

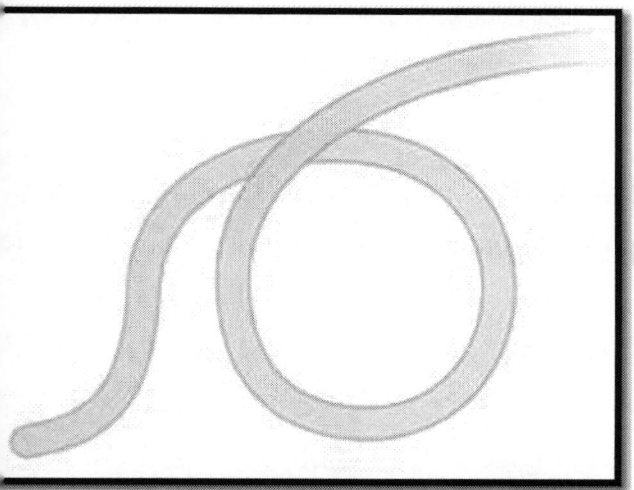

Making a circle with yarn, with the loop pointing downwards, is the easiest method.

ake a yarning circle as shown.

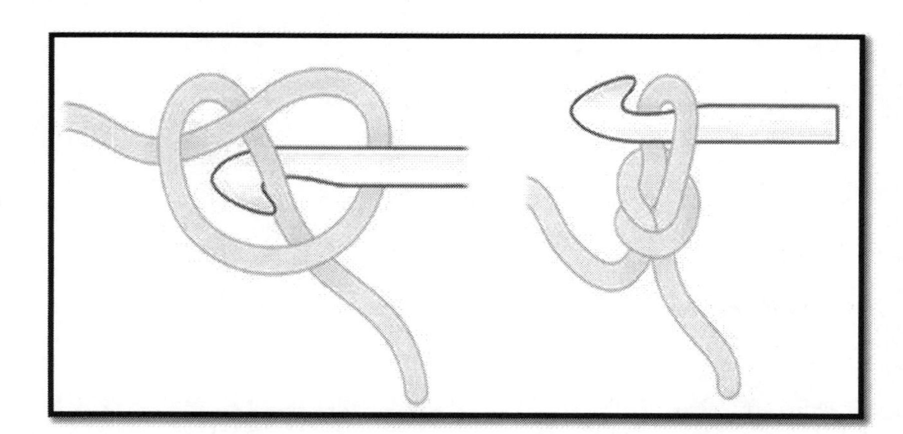

old the circle at the top of the loop where the yarn crosses in one hand and let the tail fall the rear so that it falls over the loop's center. Pull a loop across the circle with your free and or with the tip of a crochet hook.

ull the hook gently through the loop until it creates a loose loop on a hook.

HOW TO BEGIN TO CROCHET STITCH

The process of a loop being dragged through another loop with a hook is the basis of crochet stitches. Right-handed crocheters work from right to left.

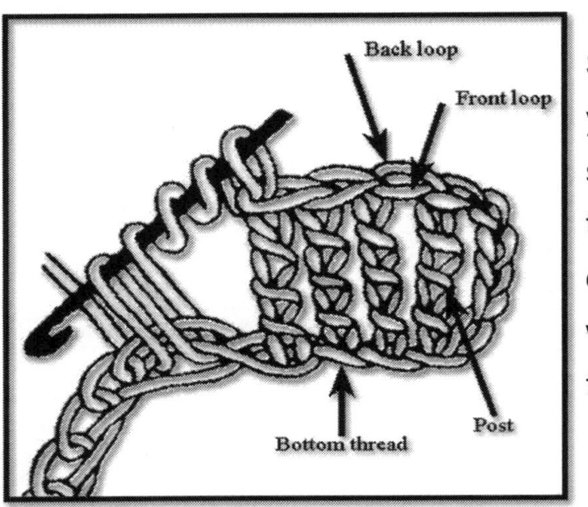

Start using 8ply yarn & 3.50mm sized hook / 4p yarn & 2.50mm sized hook while learning the b sics, so all stitches are visible. Before trying fin threads, learn the basic processes first. Unless ot erwise specified, pick up 2 top threads of each Stitc while crocheting. The front and rear loops make u the two upper threads. Follow the following steps :

Step 1.

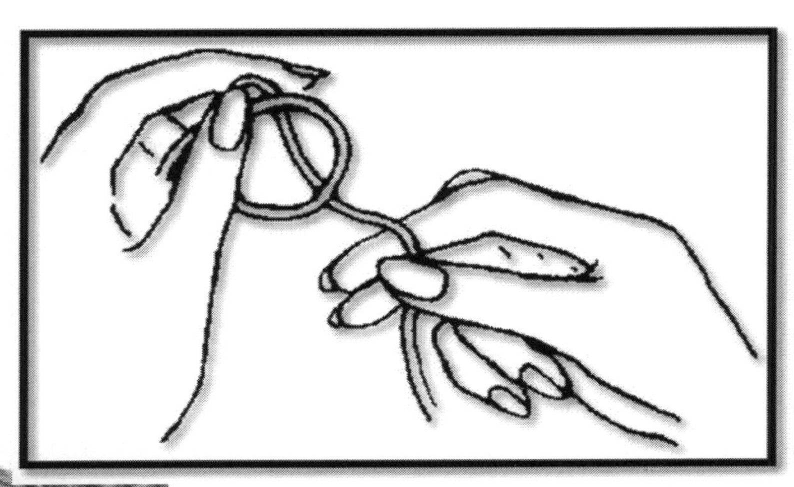

For loop making:

- Hold the thread at the end wi the left hand's thumb and forefinger.
- Make a loop with your right har by looping the long thread over a sma thread.
- Place this loop between yo thumb and fingers on your left hand.

tep 2.

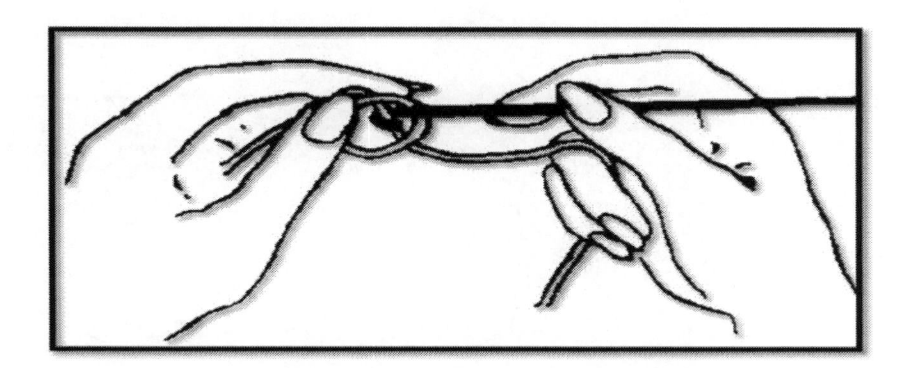

Grasp the wide bar of the hook with your right hand as if it were a pencil.

Slip the hook under a long thread and through the loop. Grasp the long end of the thread with your right hand. Draw the loop all the way through.

Don't pull the hook out of the thread.

tep 3.

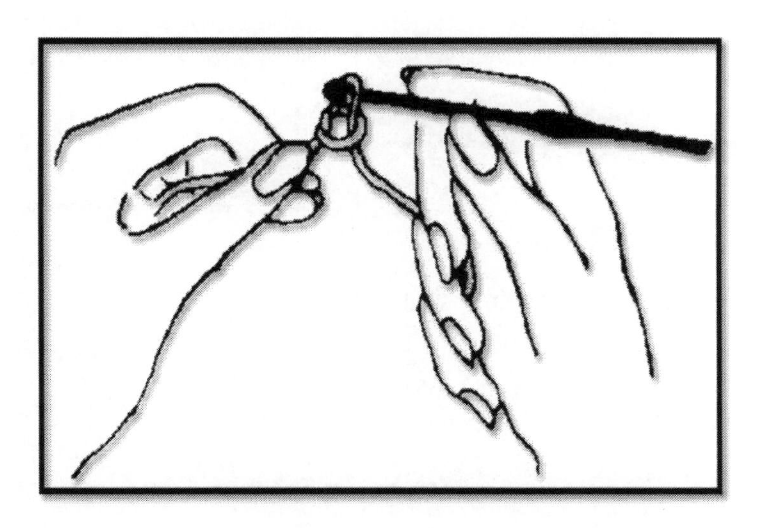

Pull the short end of the thread and ball thread in different directions to tighten the loop around the hook's end.

WHAT TO DO WITH THE LEFT HAND?

Step 4.

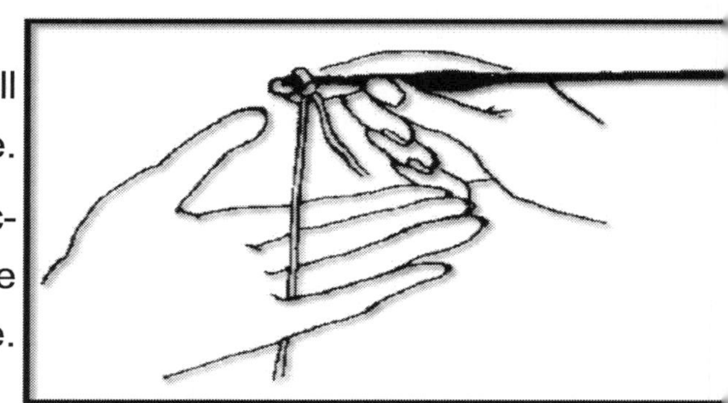

- Measure around 10cm down the ball thread from a loop on a hook using your eye.
- With the palm of a hand facing up, place the thread between the ring and little fingers around this place.

Step 5.

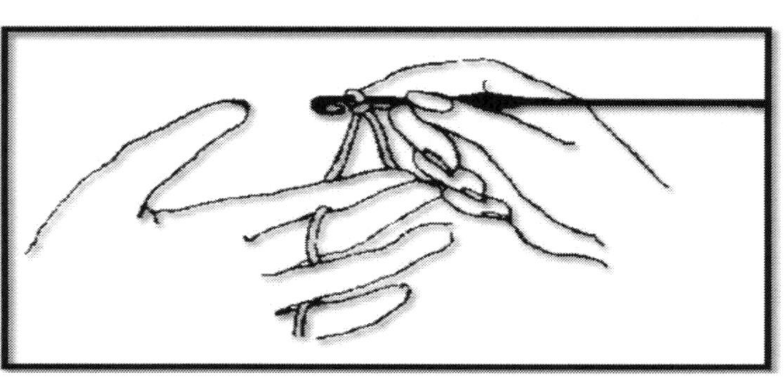

- Take the thread behind your han under your little and ring finger across your middle finger, and under your forefinger to the thum

Step 6.

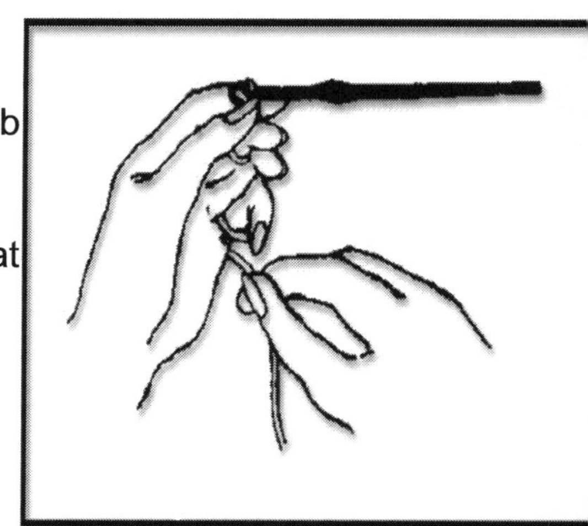

- Hold the hook and loop with the left hand's thumb and fingers.
- Gently draw the ball thread over the fingers so that it is snug but not too tight.
- Grasp the loop's knot between thumb and fingers.

WHAT TO DO WITH THE RIGHT HAND

Step 7.

- Take a pencil-like grip on the wide bar of the hook.
- Bring your middle finger forward and lay it at the hook's tip.

Step 8.

Adjust the left hand's fingers: the middle finger is bent to manage tension, while the ring and little fingers control the thread. The hook should move freely and evenly in the right hand, while the thread should move freely and evenly in the left. With time and experience, you'll be able to do it with ease.

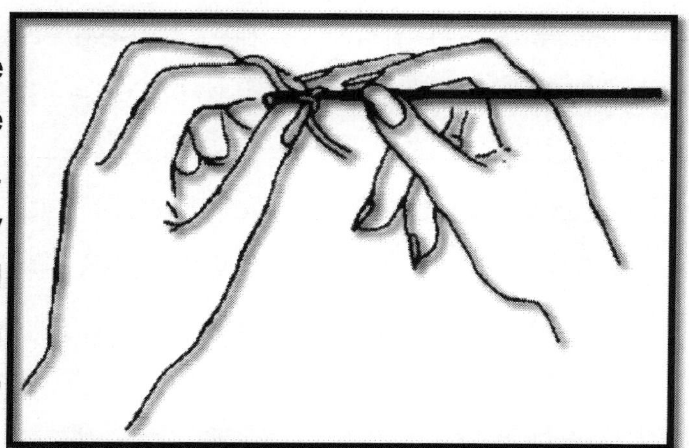

CHAIN (CH) CROCHETING

All crocheting is built on this basis. Chain is used to start crocheting, provide height at th start of a row, and design designs that need an opening or hole. Work the chain stitche looser than the subsequent rows while crocheting the first row (foundation chain).

Step 9.

- Thread the hook through the thread and grab it with the hook. The technique is known as "thread over" or "yarn over hook."
- Pull the thread through a hook's loop. This results in a single chain (ch). A stitch does nc include the loop on a hook.

Step 10.

- Rep Step 9 until you get the desired number of chains (ch) - one loop should always remain on the hook.
- Keep the thumb and forefinger of your left hand near a stitch you're working on.
- Practice chain stitches until they're all the same size.

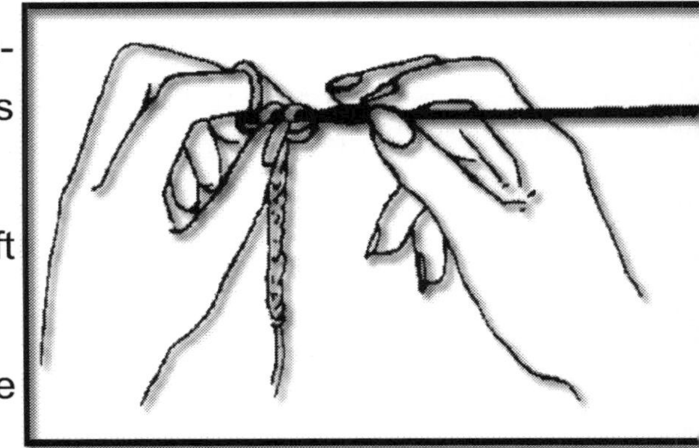

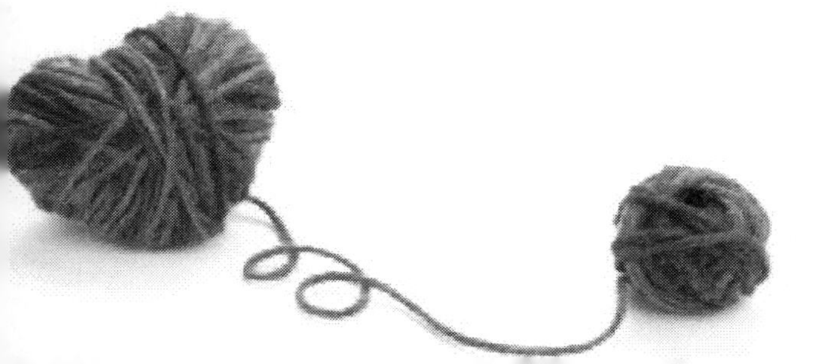

SLIP STITCH (SL ST)

n circular crocheting, slip stitching has been used to move across a row without producing epth and join rounds.

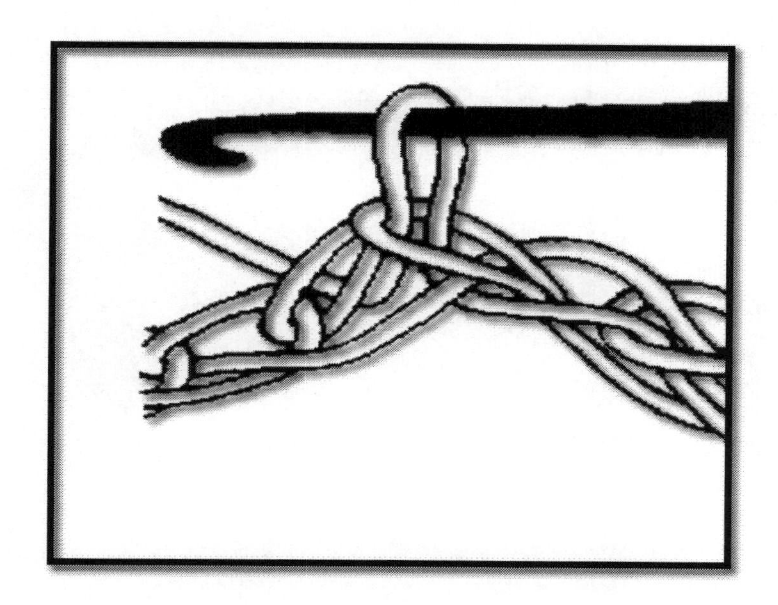

hread the hook through a stitch and loop on the hook in one movement by insert-ng it from the front, beneath the two top threads of the Stitch adjacent to the hook, reading over and drawing it through both the Stitch and the loop on the hook.

DOUBLE CROCHET (DC)

Make a chain length and hook it under two top threads of the second chain from a hoc from the front. Turn the thread over.

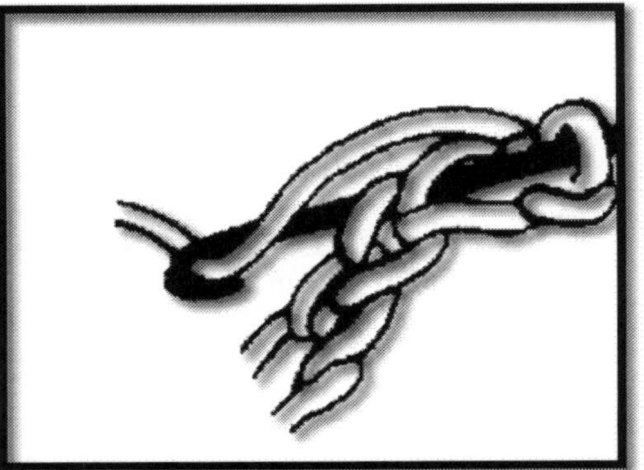

Pass it through the chain; the hook now has two loops. Turn the thread over. One loc will stay on the hook after drawing through the two loops. Now you've finished one doub Crochet (dc). Insert the hook beneath the two top threads of the next Stitch & repeat a necessary for the next dc.

HALF TREBLE (HTR)

:reate a chain length, thread it over, and hook it under the 2 top threads of the third ch om the hook, inserting from the front. Draw the thread across and through this ch. Thread ver and pull it through all three loops on the hook; one loop will stay on the hook. Comleted one-half treble (1htr). Thread over, put a hook under the 2 top threads of the next h, and continue as before for the next htr.

TREBLE (TR)

Make a chain length, thread it over, and insert a hook from the front, beneath the two to threads of the fourth ch from the hook.

Draw the thread through this ch. Thread across all three loops on the hook. Draw it throug two loops, leaving two loops on the hook, then thread it over. Draw it through the last tw loops, leaving one on the hook.

One treble (1tr) is finished. Thread over, put a hook under the 2 top threads of a next c and repeat as necessary for the next tr.

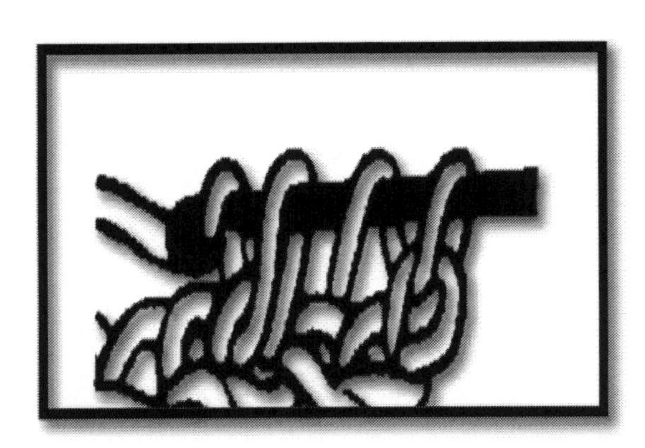

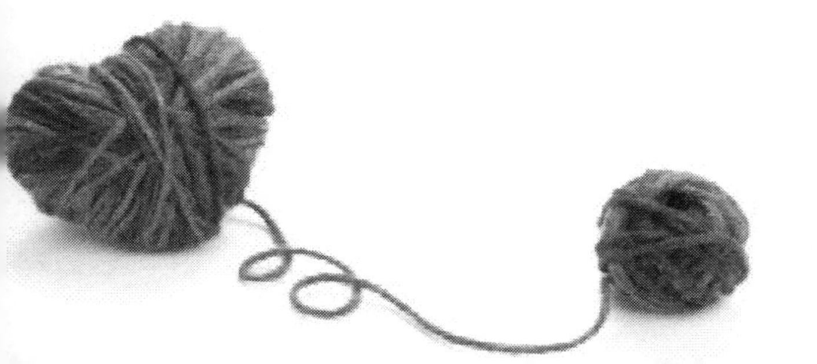

DOUBLE TREBLE (DTR)

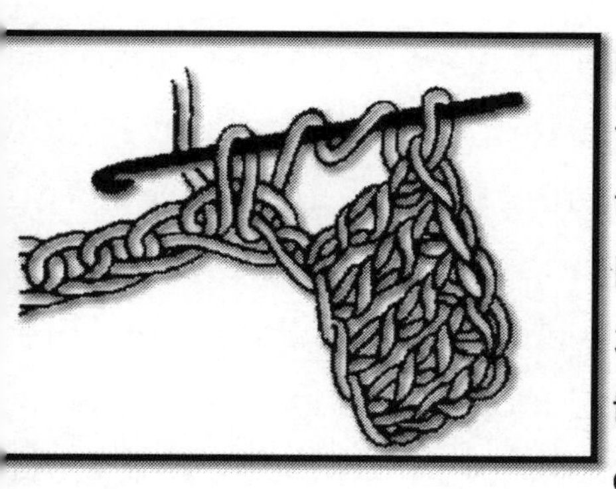

Make a chain length, thread it over twice, put a hook from the front, under the 2 top threads of a 5th ch from a hook, thread over, and pull it through the ch. There are now 4 loops on the hook; thread over and draw it through 2 loops; 3 loops will remain on the hook; thread over and draw it through 2 loops; 2 loops will remain on the hook; thread over again and draw it through the remaining 2 loops; 1 op will remain on the hook; thread over and draw it through the remaining 2 loops; 1 loop ill remain on the hook. One double treble (1dtr) has now been completed.

hread a hook under the 2 top threads of a next ch and continue as before for the next dtr.

TRIPLE TREBLE (TRIPTR)

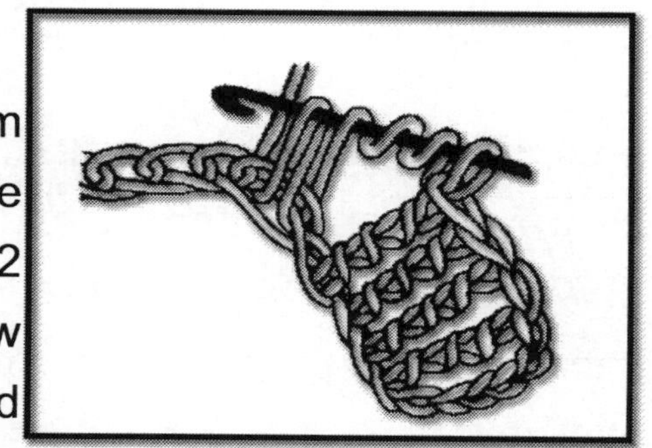

ake a chain length, thread it three times, enter the ook from the front, under the 2 top threads of a 6th ch from hook, thread it over, and pull it through the ch. There are ow 5 loops on the hook; thread over and draw it through 2 ops; 4 loops will remain on the hook; thread over and draw through 2 loops; 3 loops will remain on the hook; thread ver again and draw it through 2 loops; 2 loops will remain the hook; thread over and draw it through the remaining 2 loops; 1 loop will remain on e hook; thread over again and draw it through the remaining 2 loops; 1 loop will remain the hook; thread over and draw it through, and the first triple treble (triptr) has finally een achieved.

hread over three times, place the hook beneath the two top threads of a next ch and conue as before for the following triptr.

QUADRUPLE TREBLE (QUADTR)

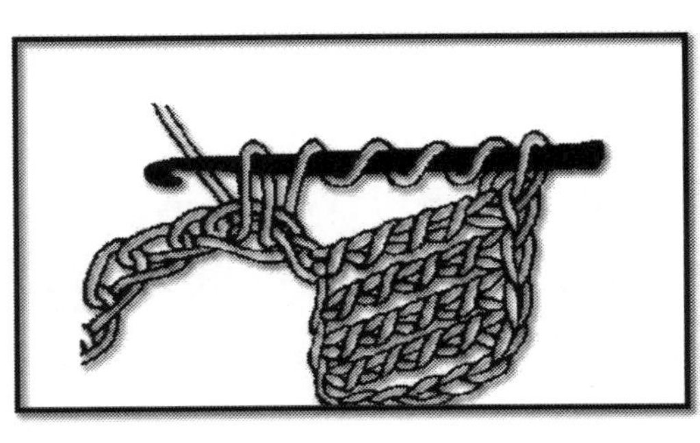

Make a chain length, thread it over four times, then put hook from the front, under the 2 top threads of a 7th c from a hook, thread over, and pull it through the ch. The are now 6 loops on the hook; thread over and draw through 2 loops; 5 loops will remain on the hook; threa over and draw it through 2 loops; 4 loops will remain c the hook; thread over and draw it through 2 loops; 3 loops will remain on the hook; threa over again and draw it through 2 loops; 2 loops will remain on the hook; thread over ar draw it through the remaining 2 loops; 1 loop will remain on the hook; thread over aga and draw it through and the first quadruple treble (1quadtr) is now finished.

Thread over four times for the next quarter, then put the hook beneath the 2 top threads a next ch and continue as previously.

QUINTUPLE TREBLE (QUINTR)

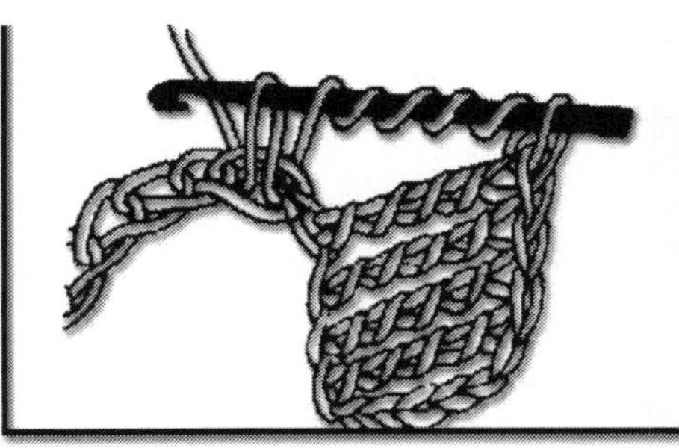

Make a chain length, thread it five times, then put the hook from the front, under the 2 top threads of an eighth ch from a hook, thread over, and pull it through a ch. There are now 7 loops on the hook; thread over and draw it through 2 loops; 6 loops will remain on the hook; thread over and draw it through 2 loops; 5 loops will remain on the hook; thread over and draw it through 2 loops; 4 loops will remain on the hook; threa over again and draw it through 2 loops; 3 loops will remain on the hook; thread over ar draw it through 2 loops; 3 loops will remain on the hook; thread over again and draw through 2 loop 1quintr, a quintuple treble, is now complete.

Thread over five times put a hook beneath the 2 top threads of a next ch, and continue a before for the next quintuple tr.

CROCHETING IN ROWS

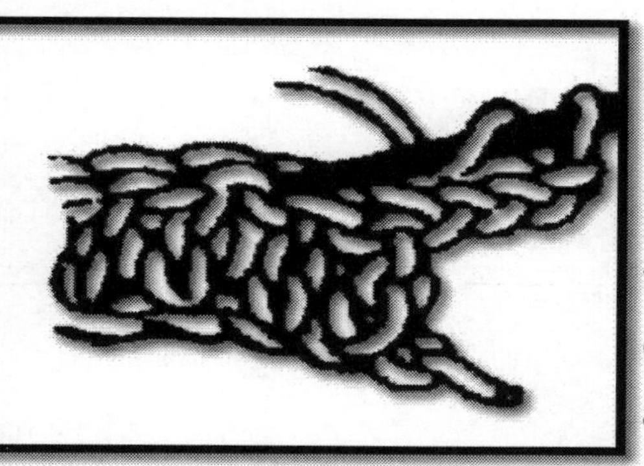

Make a chain length (foundation chain). An extra chain may be required to make the Stitch's height, depending on the Stitch to be used. Unless otherwise noted, these chains count as the initial Stitch. Some designs call for a particular number of stitches to be "missed" at the start of the first row. This also provides the necessary height. Refer to the table below for a guide. /ork a foundation row while crocheting in rows, such as trebles, then flip the work to face e reverse side after the final treble is done. Work 3 chain (turning chain) for the height, kip the preceding row's final worked Stitch and work the following treble into the top of the ext treble.

nless the pattern specifies, always place the hook beneath the 2 top threads of each titch. Carry on along the row. The row's last treble will be worked onto the top of a turning nain, a 3rd chain of the previous row's starting 3ch. Some patterns require you to work to the final Stitch of the previous row instead of the turning chain at the beginning of the w if you do not work a stitch into a turning chain at the end of a row.

The following table is solely used as a reference when calculating the number of stitche necessary for a turning chain. The number of chains might vary depending on the kind ar texture of thread & yarn used.

Rows of dc, dtr, htr, and other sts are worked in the same way, with the height of the turnir chain variable.

Stitch used in row	Turning chain
double crochet	1ch
half treble	2ch
treble	3ch
double treble	4ch
triple treble	5ch
quadruple treble	6ch
quintuple treble	7ch

BREAK OFF

It means to conclude or come to an end. Cut a thread a length of 8–10cm. Pull the cut end securely through th final remaining loop on a hook. With a blunt needle, wea the end back into the main portion of the piece.

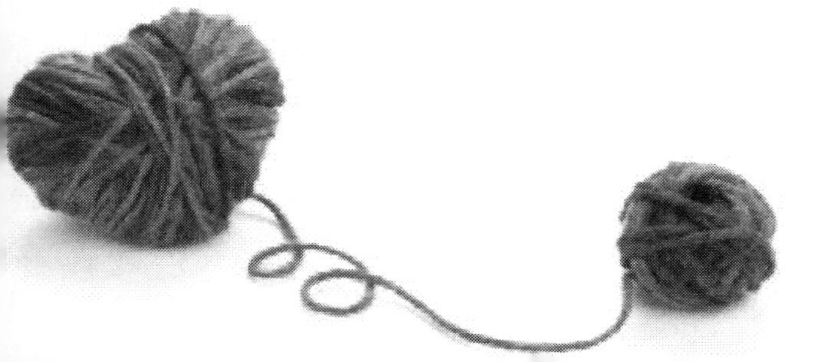

CROCHET IN ROUNDS

nless specified in the design, never turn the work between rounds while crocheting in the unds. Each Stitch is stitched beneath the 2 top threads of a preceding round's Stitch. In e crocheted item, there will be a "right side." A slip stitch (sl st) is used to link the rounds. ounds may be made in several different stitches. The next example is just in the treble. ake 4ch to begin. To construct a ring, join with a sl st into a first ch. Do not distort the ork in any way.

ound 1. 3 ch (for height & will count as 1 st). Work 11 trebles into the ring's center. Sl st to a 3rd ch of an initial 3ch to join the round (12tr)

ound 2. 3ch, 1tr in the same place as the sl st, 2tr in each of other tr, sl st into a 3rd ch a starting 3ch, join the round with the sl st into a 3rd ch of the beginning 3ch (24tr)

ne stitches must be uniformly increased in the following round, therefore continue as llows:

ound 3. 3ch, then * 2tr in the next tr, then 1tr in next tr; repeat from * to final st, 2tr in this 3ch, then Sl st into the 3rd ch of the initial 3ch to join the round (36tr). In every second itch, the increment was performed.

creasing is done by combining a certain number of stitches into a single thread. The ma- ity of patterns specify when to grow and how to do so. The goal is to keep increasing at pace that keeps the crocheting flat.

RIGHT VS. LEFT CROCHET: WHAT'S THE DIFFERENCE?

The sole difference between the right-handed Crochet and the left-handed Crochet is th hand with which you hold the hook and the direction you stitch a row. The hook is handle in the right hand in right-handed Crochet. The right-handed maker works on stitches fro right to left, with a few deviations for specialized niches of Crochet. In left-handed Croche the converse is true: the hook is held in the left hand, and the stitches are worked from le to right.

HOW TO CHANGE COLORS WHEN CROCHETING

When you're ready to change colors on a crochet project, continue the previous Stitc however, before you yarn over for the final time, drop the current color you're workir with. Place your new color on top of the crochet hook and leave the preceding color.

Pull the new color through the previous color loops, turn the project, chain 1 (for a sing chain, but if you're using double crochets or triple crochets, you'd chain two or three anc Carry on with your pattern as instructed.

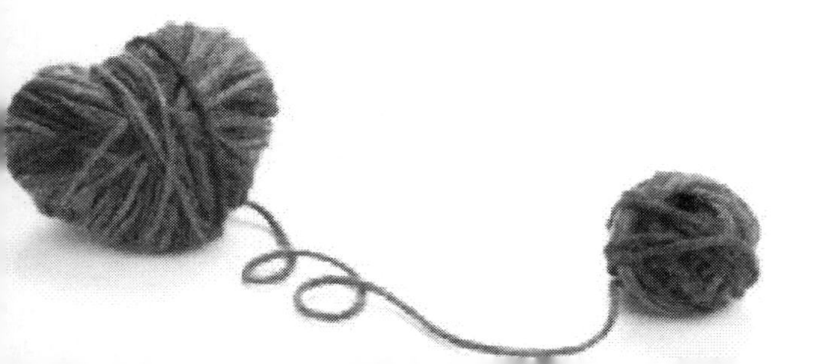

CHAPTER 4: EASY CROCHET PATTERNS FOR BEGINNERS

One of the best parts about Crochet is that you can craft beautiful, usable products ven though you're a beginner. To produce a broad range of patterns, you just need to naster a few crochet basics.

Simple rectangular shapes are used in blankets, crochet scarves, and certain shawls. You don't need to master advanced basic crochet abilities like increasing or decreasing to complete these projects. Even if you're a seasoned crocheter, beginner designs are ideal for unwinding and getting instant satisfaction from your craft.

CROCHET COWL PATTERN

Materials

- 9 MM Crochet hook
- 2 skeins of Loops & Threads Cozy Wool / 180 yards super bulky, (6) yarn
- Large Yarn Needle
- Scissors

Abbreviations

- ST = Stitch
- CH = Chain
- HDC = Half Double Crochet
- SL ST = Slip Stitch

Gauge

- 5 HDC's equals 4"

Sizing

28" circumference and 13" height that fi adults/teen

Pattern Steps:

- Round 1: Work CH 40 & SL ST initial CH to make a circle, avoidir twisting.
- Round 2: Work CH 2, HDC in third C from hook, HDC in each CH arou and SL ST to top of the first HDC. (4
- Round 3: CH 2, work HDC in the fi ST, HDC in each ST around, work S ST to first HDC's top. (40)
- Rounds 4–14: Reverse the previo round. (40)
- Finishing: Fasten off with the scisso after round 14 and weave in loo ends with a yarn needle througho the cowl.

OVERSIZED MUSTARD CROCHET SCARF

aterials

- Crochet Hook; Size Q
- 2 Skeins of Loops & Threads; Cozy Wool, Yarn in Goldenrod / any other bulky 6 yarn, i.e., Lion Brand, Wool-Ease, Thick & Quick
- Scissors
- Yarn needle

auge

- 4 DC's = 4 Inches

Pattern Steps

- Round 1: Chain 34 and attach to the first chain with the Slip Stitch to make a circle (do not twist)
- Round 2: Chain 2, Double Crochet in the same stitch and each Stitch around (34). Slip Stitch to the top of a first Double Crochet.
- Rounds 3–8: Repetition of Round 2. After Round 8, fasten off.
- Finishing: Using a yarn needle, weave in any loose ends, and you're done!!
- This cowl has a completed circumference of 36 inches and a width of 13 inches.

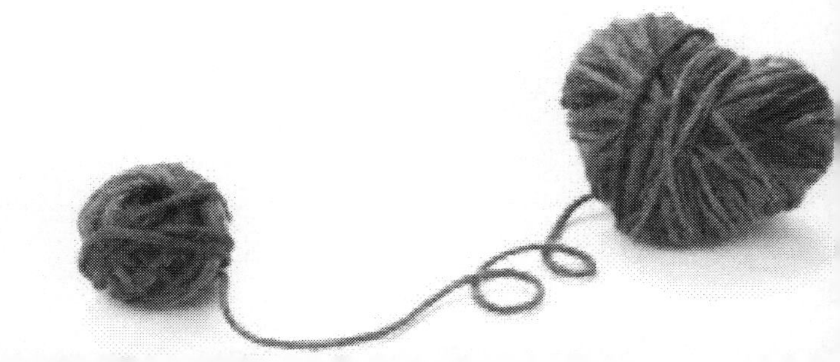

SIMPLE CROCHET WASHCLOTH PATTERN

Materials

- Size: Crochet hook H 5.00 mm
- Lily Sugar N Cream, Cotton Yarn /any worsted weight: (4) cotton yarn
- Scissors
- Yarn needle

Gauge

Approx~ 7 st's, for every 2″

Finished Size

Approx. 6″X6″; when crocheted as written

Pattern Steps

- To Begin, chain 21.
- Then starting in the 2nd CH from hook, SC, then SC in each CH acros and turn. (20)
- CH 1, then *SC in a BL of a next S then SC in an FL of the next ST, r peat from the * across to complete row, and turn. (20)
- Make a total of the 20 rows by repea ing the preceding row.
- Finishing: Fasten off, then use a ya needle to weave in loose yarn ends

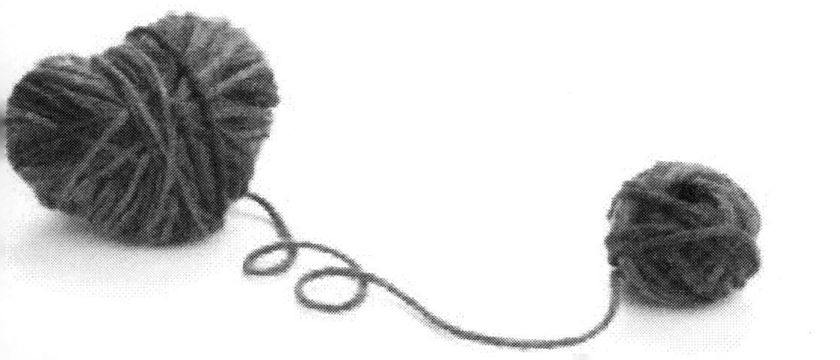

SIMPLE CROCHET BUTTON HAT PATTERN

aterials

- Lion Brand, Vanna's Choice Yarn in the Oatmeal / any worsted weight, (4) yarn.
- Clover Amour size J; 6.0 mm crochet hook,
- Yarn needle
- Large brown; 2 holes, coconut shell buttons
- Scissors

nished Size

2″ circumference (Stretches to approx. ~ 4-inch circumference) & an 8″ length

ochet Abbreviations

- DC = Double Crochet
- SC = Single Crochet
- ST = Stitch
- CH = Chain
- SL ST = Slip Stitch

Pattern Steps

- To begin: Chain 3.
- Round 1: 11 DCs in the 3rd chain from the hook, and SL ST to the first DC's top.
- Round 2: CH 2, 2 DCs in each ST around, and SL ST to the first DC's top.
- Round 3: CH 2, then *1 DC in the next ST, 2 DC in the next ST, repeat it from * around, and SL ST to the top of first DC.
- Round 4: CH 2, then * 2 DCs in the next ST, 1 DC in the next ST, then repeat from * around, then SL ST to the top of the first DC.
- Round 5: CH 2, then DC in every ST around, then SL ST to the top of the first DC.
- Round 6- 12: Repetition of round 5.
- Round 13 -15: CH 1, work SC in every ST around. Then SL ST to the top of the first SC after round 15 and Fasten off.

Finishing:

- Use yarn to attach buttons to the hat's side.
- Use a yarn needle to weave in ends throughout the hat.

KNOTTED HEADBAND CROCHET PATTERN

Materials

- Crochet hook, size; J-10 6.00 mm/ whatever hook, needed to obtain gauge.
- Lion Brand, Woolspun in the Honey/ any Bulky, (5) yarn. See the chart below for the exact yardage
- Scissors
- Yarn needle

Gauge

- 12 stitches into 9 rows = 4"
- Gauge is critical for a proper fit.

Crochet Abbreviations

- sl st = slip stitch
- hdc = half double Crochet
- ch = chain
- st = stitch

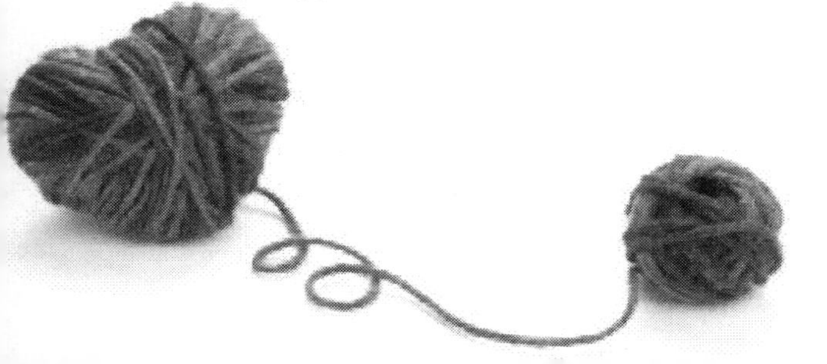

Headband Size Chart & Yardage

Sizes are listed in inches for height and ci cumference. Yarn is in yards.

	Height	Cir.	Starting Chs	Yardage
Preemie	4	9	36	42
Baby	4	14	42	56
Toddler	4	16	48	70
Child	4	18	54	85
Tween	4	20	60	99
Woman	4	21	63	106
Man	4	22	66	113

Pattern Steps

- Round 1: Ch 36 (42,48,54,60,63,66 then sl st to the first ch forming a ci cle, and making sure not to twist th ch.
- Round 2: Ch 1, work hdc in every around, then sl st to a top of the first hd NOT the ch. 36 (42,48,54,60,63,66)
- Round 3 – 9: repeat round 2.
- Finishing: keep a 12-inch strip of th yarn hanging before fastening it o To finish, squeeze the headband t gether and wrap a 12" piece around seam three or four times. Tie the ya ends together and tightly weave the into the headband.

CROCHET MITTENS

aterials:

- Men's Version: RED HEART, "Super Saver": one skein 624, Tea Leaf A
- Child's Version; RED HEART, "Super Saver": one skein, each 387, Soft Navy B & 984 Shaded, Dusk C
- Women's Version; RED HEART, "Super Saver": one skein, each 624, Tea Leaf A & 387 Soft Navy B
- Crochet Hook: 5.5mm, [US I-9]
- Yarn needle
- Stitch markers

GAUGE: check the gauge you are using. Use any size of hook to obtain a gauge. 16 sc = 4"; 17 rows = 4".

Special Abbreviation:

Sc2tog = [insert hook in the next st, yo, draw the yarn through the st] twice, yo, draw the yarn through all of 3 loops on a hook.

Pattern Steps

The directions are for a child of 4/5 years old, While the size adjustments for "women's" and "men's" are given in the parenthesis.

The child-size is 6" in diameter and 7 1/2" long. The women's size is 7 1/2" around and 11 1/2" long. The men's size is 9 1/2" around and 12" long.

Mittens:

Cuff:

Use C (B, A), and ch 15; (21, 24).

Row 1: Work in the back loops only, then sc in the 2nd ch from the hook and each ch across, then ch 1, turn.

Then repeat Row 1 for the total of 18 rows (22, 24).

Fold the cuff in half and join the ends with the slip st to form a cuff. Do not fasten it off.

Hand:

Round 1: Work along the row ends on the cuff, then slip st, evenly around for the 18 (22, 26) sts, then join the round with the slip st.

Round 2: Ch 1, place the marker, [sc in the next 8; (10, 12) sts, 2 sc in the next st] twice, Join with the slip st, [20 (24, 28) sts].

Round 3: Ch 1, [sc in the next 9 (11, 13) sts, 2 sc in the next st] twice. Join with the slip st, [22 (26, 30) sts].

Round 4: Ch 1, [sc in the next 10 (12, 14) sts, 2 sc in the next st] twice. Join with the slip st, [24 (28, 32) sts].

Child's size: Continue next step.

Women's size: Ch 1, [sc in the next 13 sts, then 2 sc in the next st] twice. Join with the slip st,(30 sts).

Men's size: Ch 1, [sc in the next 15 sts, 2 sc in the next st] twice. Join with the slip st (34 sts).

Repeat as directed, working on 1 more sc before increasing each round (38 sts).

Next Step: Continue with the stripe or solid pattern as set, for ch 1, sc in each sc around, join with the slip st. Then repeat for the total of 1 (3, 3) round.

Thumb Opening:

Next round: Ch 1, then [sc in a next 20 (2 32) sts, then ch 4 (5, 6), skip the remainir sts and then join with the slip st to first s

Upper Hand:

Sc in every st around for the 8 (10, 1 rounds; [24 (31, 38) sts], decreasing the 1 on last round for the Women's size only [(30, 38) sts].

Round 1: [Sc 10 (13, 17), sc2tog] twi [22 (28, 36) sts].

Round 2: [Sc 9 (12, 16), sc2tog] twi [20 (26, 34) sts].

Round 3: [Sc 8 (11, 15), sc2tog] twice [(24, 32) sts].

Round 4: [Sc 7 (10, 14), sc2tog] twi [16 (22, 30) sts].

Child's size only: Sc2tog around the sts), fasten off. Continue with the thumb.

Round 5: Sc in an each st around.

Round 6: [Sc 9 (13), sc2tog] twice [(28) sts].

Next 2 rounds: Then Sc2tog around [5 sts]. Fasten it off at the end of the last rour

humb:

ound 1: Join the yarn to the thumb open-
g at the st closest to the upper hand, ch 1,
: in each st around; join with the slip st [8
, 12) sts]. Sc in the each st around for 4 (7,
rounds.

ext round: Sc2tog, then sc to 3 sts from
last st, sc last for 2 sts tog [6 (7, 10) sts].
ıen Sc2tog around, working with last st as
: on a Women's size [3 (4, 5) sts]. Fasten it
'f. Weave in the ends.

HIGHLAND RIDGE PILLOW CROCHET PATTERN

Materials

- US Size; (6.5mm) K/10.5 crochet hook/ size required to obtain the gauge, 18" pillow insert yarn needle, scissors,
- Yarn: Red Heart, Soft Essentials, #5 bulky weight, yarn: 460 yards of #7305 Biscuit

Gauge

11 sts & 7 rows of pattern = 4"

Abbreviations

- ch(s) – chain(s),
- sc – single Crochet,
- dc – double Crochet,
- FPdc – front post double crochet,
- st(s) – stitch(es),
- sl st – slip Stitch,
- RS – right side

The Pattern

Row 1 (RS): Work on Ch 48, (1st 2 ch, cou as a 1 dc) 1 dc in the 3rd ch from a hook ar in each ch across; **47 dc**.

Row 2: Then Ch 2 (counts as a 1 FPdc) turn, then 1 FPdc in an each st across; 4 **FPdc**.

Row 3: Then Ch 2 (counts as a 1 dc) & tu work on 1 dc in an each st across; **47 dc**.

Row 4-31: Repeat rows 2-3.

Row 32: Repeat row 2.

Fasten off the first piece after row 32. Th after row 32 on a second piece, do not fa ten it off and then proceed to the finishi instructions.

Finishing: Hold two pieces together su that the wrong sides are in contact. On t second piece, continue with where you l off at the end of row 32: Ch 1, sc equa around three sides, passing through bo pieces.

Continue down the fourth side with the p low insert. Fasten off with an invisible link the first sc.

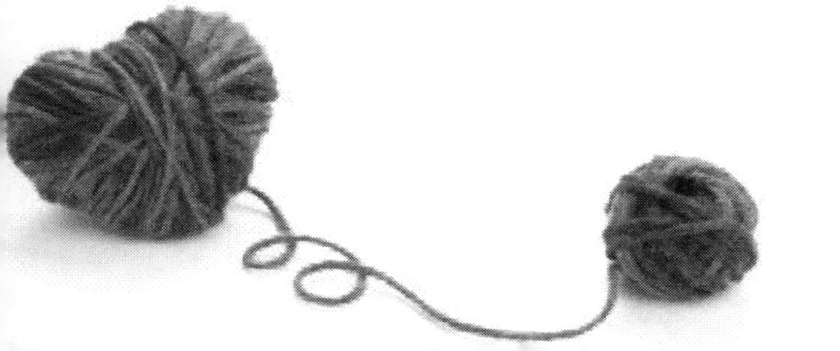

ROCHET STRIPED SUNGLASSES POUCH

aterials:

- Measuring tape
- Crochet hook size ; 5 mm / for US: H – 8 / for UK: 6.
- Needle
- Cotton Yarn; Color 1: <1 skein, Amount: approx. 22 g or 30 m or 33 yards, Color 2: <1 skein that is approx 22 g or 30 m or 33 yards
- Scissors

Gauge:

- 4 stitches & 4.5 rows per inch OR 16 stitches & 18 rows per 4 inches.
- Measured in a combination of the pattern (1 row of the hdc, 1 row of the sl st & 2 rows of a sc st).
- 1.5 stitches & 1.8 rows per cm OR 16 stitches & 18 rows per 10 cm.

Size & Measurements:

- Length: 16 cm or 6.25 inches
- Width: 9 cm or 3.5 inches

Abbreviations:

- CB = color B
- CA = color A
- Ch = chain (s)
- Prev = previous
- Hdc = half double crochet
- Sc = single crochet
- St = stitch (es)
- Sl st = slip stitch

The Pattern:

With CA work on ch 15 st.

- Row 1 with the CA: Ch 1 (counts as the 1st st), work sc 1 in all the ch from prev row, then turn (14 st).
- Row 2 with the CB: Ch 2 st, (counts as the 1st st), work hdc 1 in all the st from prev row, the turn (14 st).
- Row 3 with the CB: Ch 1 (counts as the 1st st), work sl st 1 through the back look in all the st from a prev row, then turn (14 st).
- Row 4-5 with the CA: Ch 1 (counts as the 1st st); work sc 1 in all the st from the prev row, then turn (14 st).
- Row 6-25: Repeat row 2-5; 5 times, with the respective colors.
- Row 26 with the CB: Repeat row 2.
- Row 27 with the CB: Repeat row 3.
- Row 28 with the CA: Repeat row 4-5; once.
- Row 29 with the CA: Ch 1 (counts a the 1st st); work sc 1 through bac then look all st from the prev row, tu (14 st)
- Row 30-53: Repeat row 2-5; 6 time with the respective colors.
- Row 54 with the CB: Repeat row 2.
- Row 55 with the CB: Repeat row 3.
- Row 56 with the CA: Repeat row 4-5 once.
- Fasten off and cut yarn.

Finishing:

- Tighten the threads and weave in th ends.
- Sew side seams or crochet the pouc together with the slip stitches afte folding it twice.

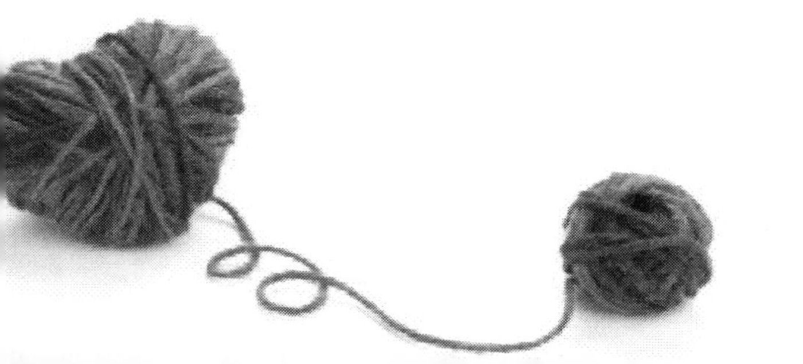

CROCHET BABY BOOTIES

aterials

- 3.0-mm Hook (D/3 USA, 11 UK)
- 3.5-mm Hook (E/4 USA, 9 UK)
- Tapestry Needle
- Sport Weight Yarn or DROPS Baby Merino in two different colors (4 PLY)

ardage

ou'll just need a small amount of yarn. or this pattern, 22 g of yarn is used for the -3-month booties & 26 g for 3–6-month aby booties.

rochet Abbreviations (Us Terms)

- BPdc – Back Post Double Crochet
- BLO – Back Loop Only
- Ch – Chain
- BPdc2tog – Back Post, Double Crochet, Two Together
- Dc – Double Crochet
- FPdc2tog; Front Post Double Crochet, Two Together
- FPdc – Front Post Double Crochet
- Sl St – Slip Stitch
- Inc – Increase
- Sc – Single Crochet
- Hdc; Half Double Crochet
- Yo – Yarn Over
- St – Stitch

Size: 0-3 Months

Length; 9 cm (3.5")

Gauge

For Gauge check that your sole measures: 3.5″ (9 cm)

Pattern Steps

Bootie Sole

Use white yarn and hook of 3.0-mm (D), ch 13.

1. Create 2 dc in the third loop from a hook. Then make 8 dc: [7 dc] all in the last loop. Work on other loops of starting chain then makes 8 dc. Then Crochet [3 dc], all in the first loop. Link with the sl st into the top loop of 2-ch spacing. (28 sts)

2. Work on Ch 2, 1 dc in same st, where you joined the previous round. Work 2 dc inc, then 8 dc, then 7 dc inc, then 8 dc, then 3 dc inc. Link by the sl st for the previous round. (42 sts)

3. Ch 1, do sc in same st, then 1 sc inc; (1 sc, 1 sc inc) twice, then 3 sc, then 2 hdc, then 3 dc. (1 dc inc, 1 dc) 3 times. Do 2 dc inc, (1 dc, 1 dc inc) 3 times, then 3 dc, then 2 hdc, then 3 sc, (1 sc inc, 1 sc) 3 times. Link by the sl st into the first ch. (56 sts)

4. Ch 1, do sl st in back loops; only all around. (56 sts)

Body Of the Bootie

Join contrasting colors.

5. Ch 2, work on 1 dc in BLO all around; (56 sts)

6. Ch 1; work (4 FPdc, 4 BPdc) for the 7 times. Link by sl st into first st; (56 sts)

7. Ch 1, work (do FPdc, FPdc2tog, FPdc, then BPdc, BPdc2tog, again BPdc); for the 7 times. Link by the sl st into the first st. (42 sts)

8. Work Ch 1, work (BPdc, then BPdc2tog, FPdc, then FPdc2tog); for the 7 times. Link by the sl st into the first st; (28 sts)

9. Work Ch 1 (2 BPdc and 2 FPdc); for th three times. BPdc2tog, then FPdc2tog. BPdc and 2 FPdc); for the 3 times. Link b the sl st into first st; (26 sts).

10. Work Ch 1, (2 BPdc and 2 FPdc); twic Work 2 FPdc. Then BPdc2tog, FP/BPd 2tog, FPdc2tog. (2 BPdc, 2 FPdc); do twice. Then 2 BPdc. Link by the sl st in first st; (23 sts)

Ankle

Switch to a 3.5-mm (E) size hook so that th bootie will be a bit softer around the ank and leg.

11. Ch 2, work dc in each st around; link sl st; (23 sts).

12. Ch 2, work dc in each st around, wi one increase, at the end (create 2 dc in la st), joined by the sl st. (24 sts)

Turn your work around, so you're croche ing in the opposite direction of what you' been doing. If not, flip the bootie inside o and keep crocheting in the same manner.

13. Ch 1, (3 FPdc, 3 BPdc); all around. Li by sl st; (24 sts).

14. Repeat the round 13; (24 sts). The wh yarn is attached again.

15. Ch 1, work sc in each st; all around, li by sl st; (24 sts). Fasten off the ends.

CROCHET MUG HUG AND RUG

aterials

- Crochet hook; 4mm hook or in a suitable size.
- Cotton yarn/ any other yarn that does not felt when washed.
- Large darning needle; for sewing.
- Two buttons.
- Pair of scissors.
- Threading needle.
- Sewing thread; to attach buttons.

auge

STS = 1"

ze

s standard 10 oz coffee mugs.

Pattern Steps

Crochet the Mug Rug

Begin by making a slip knot on your hook. Chain No. 16 Little bumps may be seen on the rear of your chain, whereas 'v' shapes can be seen on the front of the chain. Our initial row will be crocheted into the bumps on the backside. Crochet 15 single crochets until the chain is complete. Chain 1 and turn your work when you approach the end of the row. The additional chain aids in turning and neatening the edges.

Continue working 15sc rows, chaining 1 it after every row, unless you have 15 rows. Using your darning needle, cut the yarn and stitch in the ends. Don't worry if the square is a little crooked; the next edging will help straighten it up. Crochet the mug rug's border with a different color yarn now. Begin by making a slip knot on the hook and doing single Crochet on one of the square's sides. Chain 1, skip a stitch, single Crochet.

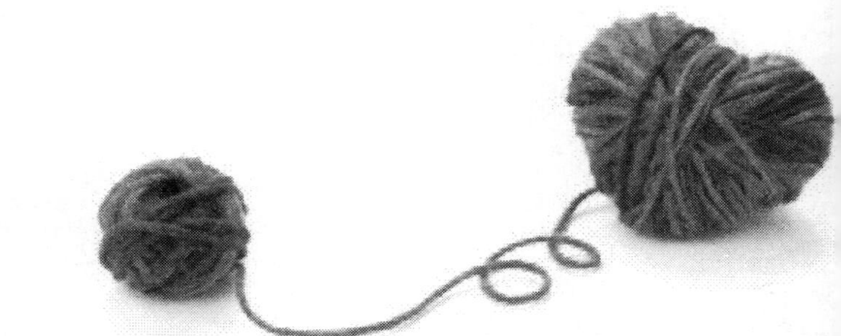

Make a single crochet in the corner, chain 1, then create another single crochet in the same Stitch. Then make your next single Crochet by chaining 1, skipping a stitch. Slip Stitch into the first single Crochet of the round to complete the circle. Make another round in the same manner with a different color, but this time work the single crochets into chain 1 spaces from the previous round. The seed stitch is the name for this technique. Continue with the seed stitch for two more rows, concluding with the final row in the same colors as your mug rug's centerpiece.

Crochet the Mug Hug

Chain 31 starts with a slip knot on the hook. Make 28 double crochets in the bumps on the back of the chain (extra three chains for turning).

Turn your work after chaining three time In the same Stitch as that of chain 3, wo the next double Crochet. Double Crochet the end of the row, then increase by crea ing two double crochets in the same Stit in the last Stitch. Continue in this mann until you've completed 5 rows of dcs with a increase at the beginning and end of ea row. Work the double Crochet through ea Stitch until you approach the end, without i creasing. In the final Stitch, do not increas There are now six rows.

Finish off our work with a single crochet bo der. This is the corner; work 3 single croche across the double Crochet that is curren on. Continue working 2 single crochets ov each double Crochet till you reach the ne corner. Make three single crochet stitche Now that you've reached the original begi ning chain, Single Crochet into the 'V' forr until you've reached the end. To make t button loop, work 2 single crochets arou the next double Crochet and chain 20. finish the corner, work another single c chet in the same space. In each of the f lowing two double crochets, add two mo single crochets. Chain 17 to make a seco button loop when you reach the final ro nish your border by crocheting 3 single ochets in the corner & 1 single crochet in ach Stitch after that. Pull up a loop between e first and second double Crochet of a top w with a different yarn color. Pull up a loop pull through the loop on your hook with ur hook in between the next two stitches. ontinue slipping stitching around the next itch until you come to the end of the row.

sing the slip stitch, make two additional ripes. Sew on the buttons using your two ttons, sewing thread and threading nee-e. Make sure they're in the corners of your ork. Now is the moment to stitch in any maining ends. Sew the ends in with your arning needle. It's typically a good idea to troduce the ends of your work to the rear d stitch them in there, so they're hidden om view.

EASY CROCHET BASKET

Materials

- crochet hook, size H (5.00mm) / size needed to have a gauge
- approximately 200 yards, of bulky/ 315 yards of super bulky yarn
- tapestry needle & scissors
- stitch marker

Size & Gauge:

Rounds 1-9= 4" ; diameter circle (bulky) / 5.5" diameter circle; (super bulky), Finished basket measures approximately 10" wide & 6" high (bulky) / 11.5" wide & 8" high (super bulky)

Pattern Steps:

- With Color A, create a magic loop.
- Round 1: ch 1, work sc 6 into t magic loop, and pull it tight. (6)
- Round 2: work directly into first st previous round, work 2sc in each around; (12)
- Round 3: work *2sc in the first st, wo sc in the next st, then repeat from around. (18)
- Round 4: work *2sc in the first st, wo sc 2, repeat the * around. (24)
- Round 5: work *2sc in the first st, wo sc 3, repeat from the * around. (30)
- Round 6: work *2sc in the first st, wo sc 4, repeat the * around. (36)
- Round 7: Work *2sc in the first work sc 5, repeat from the* aroun (42)
- Round 8: Work *2sc in the first work sc 6, repeat from the * aroun (48)
- Round 9: Work *2sc in the first work sc 7, repeat the * around. (54)
- Round 10: Work*2sc in the first work sc 8, repeat from the * aroun (60)
- { note that pattern repeats, change at this point to ensure the bottom basket can be placed flat}
- Round 11: Work *sc 5, work 2sc in t

next st, work sc 4, repeat from the * around. (66)

- Round 12: Work *sc 3, work 2sc in the next st, work sc 7, repeat from the * around. (72)
- Round 13: Work *sc 9, work 2sc in the next st, work sc 2, repeat from the * around. (78)
- Round 14: Work *2sc in the first st, work sc 12, repeat from the * around. (84)
- Round 15: work *sc 7, work 2sc in the next st, work sc 6, repeat from the * around. (90)
- Round 16: work *sc 3, 2sc in the next st, work sc 11, repeat from the * around. (96)
- Round 17: Work *sc 11, work 2sc in the next st, sc 4, repeat it from the * around. (102)
- Round 18: Work *sc 6, work 2sc in the next st, work sc 10, repeat from the * around. (108)
- Slip Stitch into first st, of round 18, turn your work (the wrong side is facing you).
- Round 19: work ch 1& sl st into each stitch around. (108)
- Turn work so that the right side is facing you.
- Round 20: work ch 1, sc into each st around, work sl st to the top of the first sc. (108)
- Round 21: Work ch 1, work sc into the same st as join & in each st around, work sl st to the top of first st; (108), then *switch to Color B
- Round 22-32: Work ch 1, sc into the same st, as join & in each st around, work sl st to the top of the first st. (108); then *switch to Color C
- Round 33-41: work ch 1, work sc into the same st, as join & in each st around, work sl st to the top of the first st. (108)
- Round 42: work ch 1, sc 23, then on ch 12, sk next 8 sc, then sc 46, then to ch 12, sk next 8 sc, work sc 23, work sl st to the top of the first st. (116)
- Round 43: Work ch 1, sc 22, work sc in the next st, one row below, work hdc 16 in the chain space, work sc in the next st, one row below, work sc 44, sc in the next st, one row below, work hdc 16 in the chain space, work sc in the next st, one row below, work sc 22, use the invisible join to the end. (124). Then Fasten off & weave in the ends.

CROCHET IPHONE CASE

Materials:

- Crochet hook that is 1 size smaller than recommended, on the yarn packaging or uses 5.5mm/ US 9
- Size 5, bulky weight yarn; in 1 / 2 colors that are approx. 35 yards
- Button; your choice
- Darning needle
- Thread
- Sewing needle
- Your phone (for size)
- Scissors

Gauge

For this design, the gauge isn't important. However, it is suggested that you crochet with tight stitches.

Maintaining the tension on this casing strong, tight, and constant will have a more defined look and feel throughout the process.

Crochet Abbreviations (Us Terms)

- **sc** = single Crochet
- **sl st** = slip Stitch
- **ch**= chain

Pattern Size

Round 1:Make a slip knot and chain about to 8 chain stitches (ch). Remember to mai tain a high level of tension. When the cha is tightly stretched, the width of the cha should be the same as the width of yo phone. If you want the case to be tight, u (ch) 6, but if you want it to be a bit loos and roomier, use (ch) 7 or 8.

Round 2: Without rotating your work (sc) the second chain from the end (same end your hook) and in each Stitch back acro the row. In the final Stitch, make 2 (sc).

Round 3. Turn around the corner, so you' working into your original chain and still g ing right to left, 2 (sc) in the first Stitch, (s rest of stitches in a row except 2(sc), in fir Stitch, with your work facing you. Repeat as many rows as necessary until you ha the right width to suit your phone's bottc (about 3-5 rows, the total depends on hc snug/ roomy for your cover). Keep yc phone ready to evaluate the fit and ma sure it's comfortable.

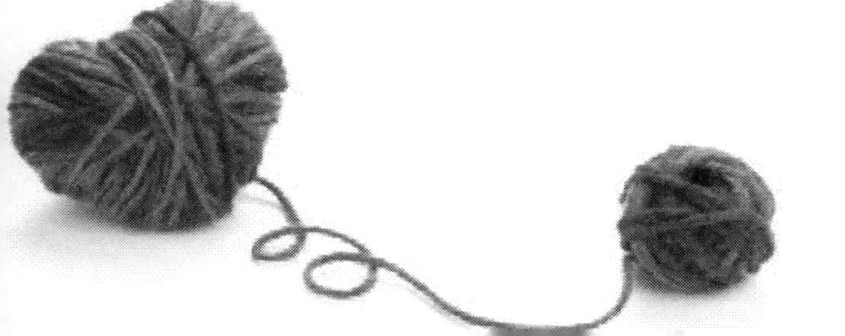

ounds 4–6: are the most difficult. Work 1 c) in each Stitch for each row until your hone reaches the top.

ast row, second to last. You have the op- n of keeping your yarn color the same or lding a second color. Begin with one more w of (sc) on one side of the case, then ift to 1 (sl st) in each

itch at the end of that row. When you get the precise center of your case, (ch) 30 tches to make a long chain, then (sl st) 1 tch in the place where your chain starts to ake a loop that will pass over the button.

ien go around the remainder of the row itil you reach the beginning. Fasten off d use your darning needle to weave in ose ends.

ll the chained loop over your phone and ace it in the case. Mark the precise area the case where the end of the loop lands, ntered on the case, then sew your button there.

is design may be used for any phone or plet by increasing the number of the stitch- at the beginning to account for the addi- nal width. These would also make excel- t presents.

TEAM SPIRIT SCRUNCHIE

Materials:

- Yarn, #4 Worsted Weight
- Hook, US Size (I/9), 5.5mm
- Other Tools: Scissors, Yarn Needle, Elastic Hair Ties

Stitches/Abbreviations: US Terms

- ch – chain
- st(s) – stitch(es)
- dc – double Crochet
- sl st – slip stitch
- blo – back loop only

Pattern Size:

Color A should be tied to the hair tie.

Round 1: work Ch 1, make 40-45 sc, arou the hair tie, join.

Round 2: Ch 2, work 4 dc in the same st the ch 2, work *3 dc in the next 2 sts, wo 4 dc in the next st; then repeat from the around; Join. Fasten it off A. (Depends the starting sc, then round count, you c end on the 3 dc, in st /4 dc in st, it does matter which one).

Round 3: Link B in same st, like join, ch in blo, sl st in the next st and the each around, link to first st, where you joined Fasten it off. Weave in the ends.

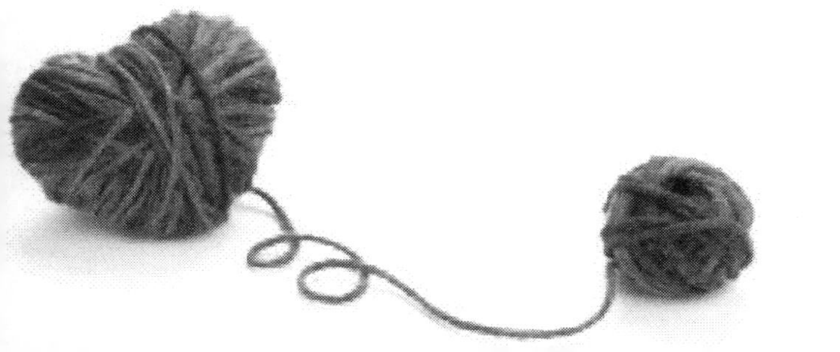

CROCHET CHICKEN - HEN & CHICKS AMIGURUMI

aterials

- Black embroidery floss or crochet thread
- Acrylic yarn in red, white, yellow, orange-pink, and twig-brown

ols

- 2.5mm hook
- 2.3mm hook
- 4mm hook
- Polyester fiberfill
- Darning needle
- Pins
- Scissors

Abbreviations

- Sc: single Crochet
- Ch: chain
- Dc: double Crochet
- Ss: slip stitch
- Inv dec: invisible decrease

Pattern Steps:

Body

Tori's body is knit quicker with two strands of yarn from two distinct balls.

Use 4mm hook and white yarn (with two separate balls of yarn)

Round 1: work Sc 6 in magic ring {6}

Round 2: work [Inc] around {12}

Round 3: work [Inc, sc 1], around {18}

Round 4: work [Inc, sc 2], around {24}

Round 5: work [Inc, sc 3] around {30}

Round 6: work [Inc, sc 4] around {36}

Round 7 – 12; (6 rounds altogether): work Sc around {36}

Round 13: work [Inv dec, sc 4] around {30}

Round 14: work [Inv dec, sc 3] around {24}

Round 15: work [Inv dec, sc 2] around {18}

Fill with stuffing

Round 16: work [Inv dec, sc 1], around {12}

Round 17: work [Inv dec], around {6}

Fasten off. Leave long strands to make eye indentations.

Beak

With the yellow yarn & 2.5mm hook

Round 1: work Sc 5 in the magic ring {5}

Round 2: work [Inc] around {10}

Fasten off & leave long end; for sewing.

Flatten the piece to resemble the triangle.

Wattle

With the red yarn & 2.5mm hook Ch 2. Sc 1.

Fasten off & leave a long end for sewing.

Comb: With the red yarn & 2.5mm hook

Surface crochet in the straight line onto the top-center of Tori's body.

Row 1: work Sc 1, ch 3, sc 2, ss into the next sc.

Row 2: work Ch 3, sc 2, ss into the next sc.

Row 3: work Ch 3, sc 2, ss into the next sc.

Fasten off & weave in ends.

Wings (Make 2)

With the white yarn (from the two differe balls of the yarn) & 4mm hook

Round 1: work Sc 3 in magic ring {3}

Round 2: work [Inc] around {6}Fasten off leave a long end for sewing.

Blushing Cheeks (Make 2)

With the pink yarn & 2.3mm yarn

Round 1: work Sc 5 in the magic ring {5}

Fasten off & leave long end for the sewin

Eye indentations

Thread the rest of the strand from the bo using a darning needle. Pull it up to a po on your body's left side, preferably bel Round 7.

Bring yarn back down to the bottom of t body with the horizontal backstitch.

To make an indentation, gently tug. Rep the other side. The indentations should about 5 stitches apart.

Bring the yarn to the bottom of the head, a knot, and clip the excess.

ssembly

ew the beak between the body's eye in-entations. Sew the wattle to the underside the beak.

sing black embroidery floss, sew on the es. Tori was made using black crochet read. Simply backstitches vertically be-een two stitches until the eyeballs are ick enough to your liking. For each eye, ughly 8 backstitches are created.

ake the blushing cheeks by sewing them . If you haven't already, surface crochet e comb onto the upper section of Tori's dy.

ew the wings on. Tori's adorable tiny feet ay be made by backstitching a down-ard-pointing arrow onto the twig-brown rn.

sing multiple strands of yarn helps cut wn on time it takes to complete your ami-rumi project.

ur amigurumi will have a super-cute ap-arance with oval eyes. Simply backstitch- vertically between two stitches until the eballs are thick enough to your taste. In-ead of embroidery floss, use durable cro-et thread.

Surface crochet is an excellent method to add little and fragile crochet pieces to a bigger body. Tori's comb is produced by chaining, single crocheting, and slip-stitching straight onto the body's top center.

Embroidery, which is used on Tori's feet, is the key to tiny feet. Simple backstitches may be used to mimic small claws. Varied hook and yarn size combinations provide different outcomes.

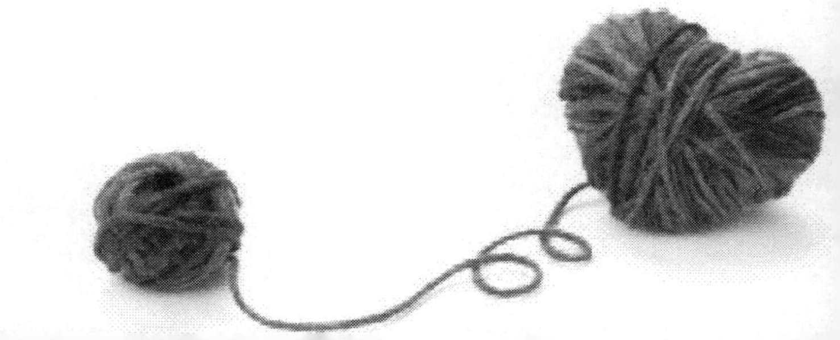

CHAPTER 5: COMMON CROCHET MISTAKES AND HOW TO SOLVE THEM

People make the same errors, whether they just started to Crochet or have years of xperience. It's quite OK to make these frequent crochet mistakes! It's better to be aware f such time suckers to prevent issues that might derail your efforts.

Here are a few common crochet mistakes and tips for how to correct or avoid them.

CROCHET IS NOT THE SAME AS KNITTING.

Crocheters have been known to refer to their work as knitting. Crochet is made with o hook, while knitting is done using two needles. Crochet hooks are often known as needle however, while crocheting, you need one.

FAILING TO MAKE A GAUGE SWATCH.

The number of stitches and rows in a 4 by 4-inch crochet fabric is referred to as gauge. T designer has included a gauge to ensure that the project has the right size. You will hate devote hours upon hours into a project to discover either it's too little or far too large wh finished.

Assume your design specifies a medium-weight yarn and I/9 sized hook. There are rows in 4 inches of cloth and twelve single crochet stitches across the 4 inches. Compa the figures (if available) to the pattern's gauge. You're good to go if they're pretty near match. If not, you'll need to adjust the tension or switch to new hook size. Granted, not crafts need a gauge, but it's critical if you're producing clothing.

CROCHETING ONLY IN THE FRONT LOOP

It's simple to make this error if you're new at crocheting. Understanding where to set t hook in each Stitch, this craft is the basis. This error might occur because you didn't co pletely comprehend how to crochet or maybe because your hook slips occasionally, a you aren't experienced enough to recognize the error straight away. Spending additio time examining each row that you work is a great strategy to correct this error. It may se tiresome at first, but now that you've learned the basic rule of crocheting under both loo you should double-check your stitches until their second nature.

YOUR PROJECT KEEPS GETTING WIDER

is is a common blunder that everyone does at some point. When you start a certain oject, you consider it so simple and think that it's just repeating the same Stitch back and rth. After an hour, you see that your rectangular blanket has turned into a hexagon!

is problem arises when you don't count your stitches and end up working extra stitches an necessary. You might be doubling up into one Stitch or working a stitch inside the turn- g chain accidentally. The best way to avoid making this error is to count your stitches! You ay either count each row as you complete it or keep a careful eye on the overall form of ur work. Don't lose time working rapidly to discover that you added Stitch 10 rows back.

YOU AREN'T CHECKING YOUR ROWS WHILE WORKING

is point, like the one before it, is all about not squandering your all-too-valuable time. u must count the rows in the same way that you must count your stitches while crochet- g. Using a row counter is the simplest answer to this issue. That may be a smart digital w counter which counts each row with a single click, or you could go back to basics using en and notebook to make a tiny tick after each completed row.

CONFUSING U.S. AND U.K. CROCHET TERMS

Because there are so many patterns accessible online, you may find them termed in U terms. That's fantastic if you're from the U.K., but you should be aware that the words diff from the U.S. to the U.K. if you're from the U.S. Single crochet in the United States is t same as double Crochet in the United Kingdom.

U.S. Terms		UK Terms	
Slip Stitch	Sl st	Slip Stitch	Ss
Chain	Ch	Chain	Ch
Half double crochet	Hdc	Half treble	Htr
Single Crochet	Sc	Double Crochet	Dc
Treble Crochet	Trb	Double Crochet	dtr
Double Crochet	(Dc	Treble	Tr

When it comes to working patterns, you will observe how that might make a differen Use this table to convert terminology from the United Kingdom to the United States.

USING A DIFFERENT YARN WEIGHT AND EXPECTING THE SAME RESULT AS THE PATTER

When it comes to following a crochet pattern, the yarn weight is really important. If y want to make a bulky scarf out of a pattern that calls for #6 yarn, but you only have a # your gauge will be different, and your completed item will appear different.

Each pattern is written with a certain yarn in mind, and even a small weight adjustme might influence the result. It is recommended to do your gauge swatch if you are usi up the yarn you have on hand. This will define what changes to the pattern you'll need make to get it as near as possible.

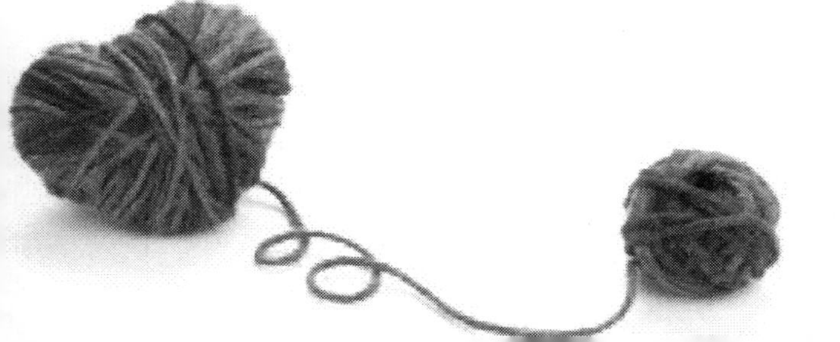

USING AN INCORRECT HOOK SIZE

is and the previous points are both common blunders. Using the incorrect hook size may have significant impact on the result of your project. Each pattern is designed with a certain hook size mind and altering it will result in stitches that are either too tight or too loose.

ake sure you read the pattern carefully to ensure you're using the appropriate size. Also, don't rget to create your gauge swatch! You may not even know you're holding the incorrect hook, but you see your gauge swatch is inaccurate, you've just saved yourself a lot more time frogging a hole work!

NOT READING THE ENTIRE CROCHET PATTERN BEFORE STARTING

e most important thing you have to do when beginning a new project is going over each line. All u have to do now is take your yarn and hook and get started! After getting some experience in rking with crochet patterns, you will note that not reading the pattern first is a mistake. However, it may not make a significant difference every time.

s a good idea to read the design prior so you can master a new stitch ahead of time. Although you n't have to remember each step, reading through a pattern is similar to preparing for an exam fore taking it. It's always preferable to get right into a new crochet project!

CORRECTLY COUNTING THE STARTING CHAIN/NOT KNOWING WHERE TO PLACE THE FIRST STITCH

e starting chain is the basis of any crochet project (possibly one of the least pleasurable aspects). aining is one of the first tasks you'll learn to crochet, and it's also one of the most difficult.

e of the most frequent mistakes is not putting the initial Stitch in the correct chain when chain-. This will result in either too many or too few stitches, and if you aren't counting them, your oject will be doomed from the beginning. The easiest approach to prevent or solve this issue is get very familiar with chaining and counting chains.

Failure to Leave a Long Enough Yarn Tail

Probably everyone's least favorite aspect of crocheting is weaving in the ends. No, y can't just snip the yarn and hope no one notices, only to struggle later because your stra is too short.

It doesn't matter whether you're adding a new ball of yarn, binding off a project, or tra sitioning between different colors of yarn; you need to allow enough length to weave Leaving at least 5-6 inches of yarn is recommended to make this procedure as easy possible.

CROCHETING TOO LOOSELY OR TOO FIRMLY OR ALTERING THE TENSION.

It's important to maintain a constant level of tension. Taking your time is one method to this. It's more important to focus on making neat even stitches; speed will come later. Yo have difficulty working the following row if you crochet them too tightly since you'll be stru gling with the hook to get it into the stitches. Your gauge will be incorrect if you crochet t loosely, and your work will appear sloppy. Your whole product will be uneven and crook if your tension fluctuates a lot.

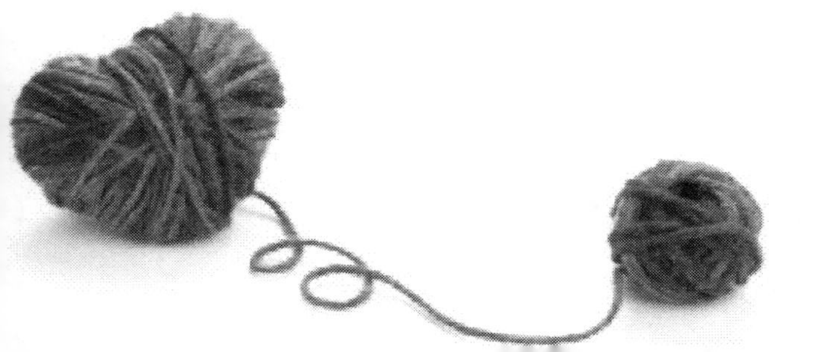

YOUR PROJECT'S SIDES GROW OR SHRINK.

is is a relatively frequent mistake made by newcomers. Knowing where to work the first tch of each row, the final Stitch, and how many chain stitches to do at the beginning of ch row are the keys to having good even edges.

e following are the rules for starting each row:

- 1 chain stitch in single Crochet
- 2 chain stitches in half double Crochet
- 3 chain stitches in double Crochet
- 5 chain stitches in treble or triple Crochet

t the last Stitch into the preceding row's top chain stitch. Make it a habit to count your tches throughout a row as well. You'll always end up with attractive even sides if you rt and stop at the precise locations and count stitches.

is list will be useful in your crochet journey. Always keep in mind that you are not alone making crochet errors and that you will be able to look back and grin at how far you have ne over time!

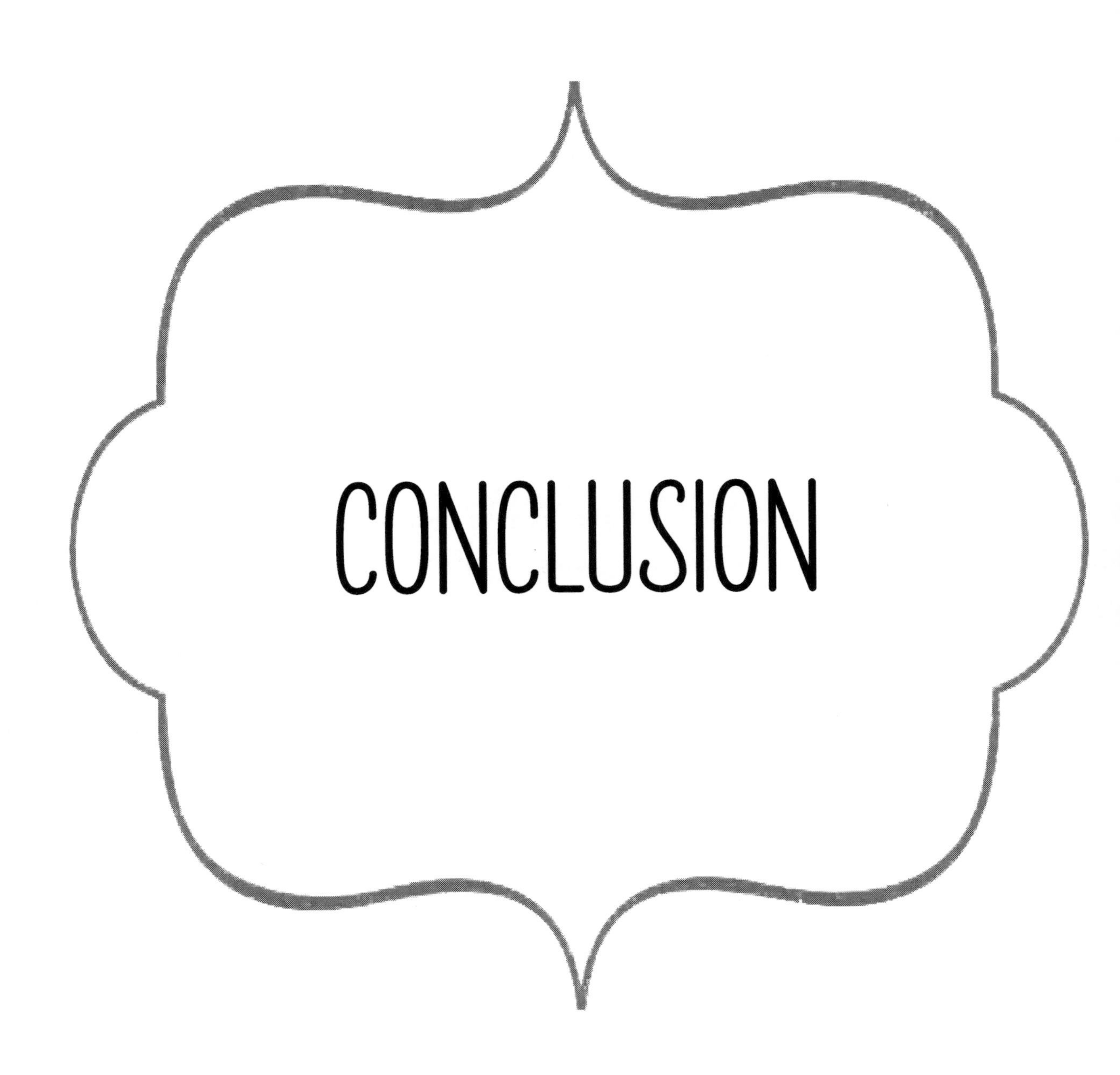

CONCLUSION

Crochet for beginners is a book that teaches you how to crochet if you've never done it fore. You'll learn all you need to know about the equipment and materials you'll need, as ll as how to utilize them. Crochet and pattern language might be difficult to understand times, but this book has simplified it for you so you can pick it up fast and start crocheting ht away. Basic stitches are essential when learning to Crochet, and you can learn every-ng about them right here. You are free to practice as much as you like and at your speed.

nce you've mastered these stitches, you may go on to more advanced methods and ch learning. There is a guide for both left and right-handers. You'll be able to improve ur crochet abilities as you go along, and you'll be able to change your motions as you e your crochet hook to establish a rhythm. Working with yarns might be challenging at es, but you'll get the hang of it. Some helpful crochet tips and methods to make the pro-ss go more smoothly are included in this book for you. Making mistakes is challenging cause you must learn from them. However, the most common crochet blunders and the st strategies to prevent them are mentioned. You may start with basic designs utilizing a ge of stitches discussed in this book after you get going and feel secure enough to try some patterns. Once you're ready, you may take it a step further and try some more icate patterns. There are a few intermediate and advanced designs that employ stitches u'll become used to. So, best of luck! Crochet books have exploded in popularity. They written by many writers and include a variety of topics. They all have something dis-tive to give away. Thank you for including this book on your reading list, even though re are so many others.

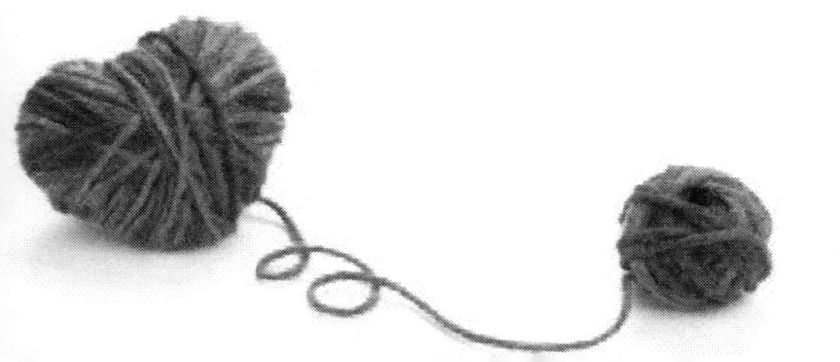

Made in the USA
Las Vegas, NV
22 March 2023